TheRhyze!, Inc. Presents

Presents

Let Go of Your But!
A Woman's Guide to Loving Herself to Full Potential and Possibility.

Naje Badu

ISBN #: 978-0-578-48677-2

All rights reserved. No part of this book may be produced by any mechanical, photographic, or electronic process, or in the form of a video recording; nor may it be stored in a retrieval system, transmitted, or otherwise be copied for public or private use - other than for "fair use" as brief quotations embodied in articles and reviews – without prior written permission of the publisher.

The intent of the author is only to offer information of a general nature to help you on your quest for emotional and spiritual well-being. In the event that you use any of the information in this book for yourself, which is your constitutional right, the author and Hampton Publishing assume no responsibility for your actions.

Cover Design: Precise Hallan
Editors: Kelsi Cunningham & Heather Nysewander

1st – 3rd Edition Publisher: Hampton Publishing
4th Edition Publisher: *TheRhyze* Inc. www.TheRbyze.com

Affirmations of Self-Love

I AM.
I EXIST.
I AM alive.
I AM all there is.
I AM unlimited potential.
I AM greater than any fear or challenge.
I AM more than any illness and discomfort.
I AM the power to create my life exactly as I envision.
I AM worthy of love, joy, friendship and healthy relationships.
I AM each decision I make because I am mindfully aligned with Truth.
I AM moving forward, continuously seeking and sharing positive energy.
I AM always capable of going above all that impedes my flow of abundance.
I AM accountable for learning and growing through whatever Life provides.
I AM Free.
I AM Truth.
I AM Love.
I AM Wise.
I AM Peace.
I AM Joyful.
I AM great *just as* I AM.
I AM rooted in mindfulness.
I AM open to embrace change.
I AM exactly what I choose to be.
I AM and have everything I need, right now.
I AM always the relationship I maintain with others.
TODAY, I patiently nurture seeds that will become the tree of my tomorrow.

A Note to My Sisters: Be aware that the content throughout this series gets progressively more challenging with each chapter. Expect the same with subsequent volumes. Know in advance that the redundancy and repetition of the messaging woven throughout its context is intentional. The *Let Go of Your But!* series has been designed in this fashion to incrementally raise the consciousness of women who are ready to transcend limitation and create new possibilities in their lives. The overall objective is to empower you to grow new roots as you endeavor the journey toward your true self and calling. New thought teacher, Neville Goddard suggests that we "do not waste one moment in regret. For to think feelingly of the mistakes of the past is to re-infect yourself." This series is designed to help you focus on the path of healing, enlightenment, fulfillment, and the fruition of your greatest aspirations.

Table of Contents

Acknowledging Women of Power	7
Our Journey…	9
What Really Matters… A Story of Inspiration	22
Understanding Your "Why?"	30
Tilling the Mind	45
Beginning with Love	59
Love's Law	72
The Four A's	83
Growing in Grace	98
Sowing Seeds (Choices)	111
Setting the Stage	122
Your Journey Begins Here	131
Rising from Within	139
Taking Time	158
Continuing the Course	177
About the Author	181

Acknowledging Women of Power

Let Go of Your But! was created in memory of a beloved angel, Kimberly Harpe. I pray you are somewhere smiling down on me and this physical world from which you transcended. I felt compelled to start a series like this because it was through you that I was able to witness a living example of how one can find joy in all things and people encountered throughout the time between their first and last breaths. Now that you have your wings, I too can smile wide, knowing that you are *everywhere* in the Universe spreading kindness, sharing love, singing your heart out, and living life as you aspired while you were here. I only wish you were here to see the changes that have manifest in my own life after your departure. I miss you!

Kimberly E. Banks, the former version of myself that got me through all the tough times that led me to where I am today. I dedicate this 4th edition of this book to you, for it is your presence, love, and support that got me to realize that as long as I am still alive, there is always time to realize a dream. Sometimes we need reminders of God's promise that our gifts and talents will make room for us. You have been strong, resilient, and intentional with your willingness to thrive. And for that I can only say, "Thank You." Even during dark times, it was you who held on to me and promised a better way toward the light. You were *that* flicker of hope and inspiration I needed when I was emerging from "my dark time." You were, and still are, the reflection I needed to see myself as I truly am, rather than what I was not or had yet to become. Thankfully, I have been recharged to continue carrying out my purpose so that I might be the model of the change I wish to see in this world.

Barbara Dyce and Angela Burris, thanks for lifting me up in light and love, and in every way I could possibly imagine. Your increasing belief in me means more to me than words can express. Though you are not always in my presence, your willingness to support me in being more of who I really am is greatly appreciated.

To my beloved twin-baby sister, Karin, thanks so much for being you. For the better part of our lives we have shared and learned lessons of strength and perseverance that will forever keep us together – in spirit and in heart…even when it doesn't feel like it.

And…to the most important woman in my world, Rena DeJarnette. It is through your willingness to step into the role of Mother that I even exist. Thank you! I wish you knew just how much I believed that it would be impossible for me to be who I am today without you. Thanks for stepping up and contributing to my purpose, as well as, all of the time and energy you spent instilling within me the will to strive and persevere. Who knew I would be here today.

And to all the women who have encouraged me to "rise up," dust off my bottom, and pursue my dreams, thanks to you as well for believing in me. I genuinely appreciate you continuing to shed light on my shortcomings, as well as holding me accountable for "walking the walk," even when I couldn't see the things you recognized in me. Immense gratitude is what I offer you in return for pushing me to *let go of my own buts* when the roads got tough.

Namaste!

Our Journey...

*I*t has taken me several years to allow this project to come into fruition exactly *as it meant to be.* There have been several revisions (we are now on the 4th edition, not to mention all the times it has been edited and re-edited over the years) and attempts to publish this book, all of which include new lessons and tiny nuggets of wisdom I am fortunate enough to have attained throughout the evolution of my life. Through all of the many revisions, the most interesting pattern I noticed was how each time I sat back in celebration of declaring this book "completed," another extremely monumental life event would arise, as if to provide me deeper insight into what it truly means to be successful, fulfilled, free, or happy – or not. I am utterly excited about sharing with you the many lessons and moments of enlightenment, along with various philosophies and perspectives that have led me toward a greater understanding of what it means to love myself fully. I now know this to be the greatest step to take in the quest for reaching my potential.

This volume is the first installation of a series that will hopefully inspire you to *let go of the buts* that somehow hinder progress and fruition in your own life. The topics within this series range from cultivating self-love, health and wellness to overcoming excuses to leadership to developing greatness to reaching full potential to building healthy, loving relationships. I have come to learn that these how we develop these facets of life contribute greatly to the beliefs we hold about our ability to achieve, as well as create the realities we desire. For that reason, there are underlying messages woven throughout the context of each chapter that will help you to understand just how immense the process of 1) getting to know who you *really are,* and 2) getting realigned with who *you are meant to be,* greatly impacts your journey of becoming more of who you already are inside.

It's all a part of the process of becoming exactly who you need to be in order to make your way toward the preferred side of your goals and life vision. Without such understanding, it is almost impossible to develop new habits that will move you from stagnation to success. None of this is possible if you aren't first cognizant about who you are being today and how much out of alignment you may be with what is true for you. So, this series is also designed to help shed light on traits, emotions, thought processes, perceptions, beliefs, choices and decisions that are potentially the root causes to the struggles you encounter in life.

I have committed myself to the lifelong endeavor of striving to be the best version of me, as well as, using the fruits of my learning to inspire others to do the same. Of course, learning for me will not stop simply because I have chosen to write a book and share it with you. Attempting to reach greatness means that I must remain a student of life. Teaching also affords me the chance to learn from you what is required to continuously stretch and expand. Consequently, this journey of evolution will not include just yourself. Nor will it be exclusively directed toward me. It will be a joint venture, one that we will amble along, together, patiently and compassionately. The motive behind this joint effort is to keep myself included in the oneness of womanhood as we continue to learn, grow, and expand. I choose to reach back, share, and contribute to the collective by way of passing on wisdom, love, and positive energy. It is my belief that as I extend insights obtained in my respective journey, I will meet other women along the way that are endeavoring to fulfill their own purpose of sharing lessons as well. Vowing to uphold the "each one, teach one" pledge, we must remain open to absorbing, cultivating and transforming.

Understand one thing: you are partly responsible for the calling forth of this book as it exists before you today. The fact that *we* (author, readers, and listeners) are all connected – in spirit and heart –

means that each of us has a contributing factor in the crossing of paths in this *exact* moment. This is resultant of the merging of *your* individual yearning to love ourselves into potential and the possibility, with *my* intention to share insights imparted unto me, and ultimately, *our* collective aspiration to grow into the best version of ourselves. I am merely an instrument being used to materialize our individual and collective vigor in the form of a book, which will hopefully serve as the tool that will propel you forward into the life you envision. Understand that the context you are about to intake was already available - to you and me - before it even appeared on a page. Thus, the alignment of our collective thoughts triggered the miraculous manifestation of what you need at this stage of your life. Your desire to love yourself fully *is* the driving force that compelled me to keep writing, to keep tapping in to my potential and creativity, to keep focusing on my desire to share and inspire women around the world.

During our time together, I will wholeheartedly support your endeavor to overcome the excuses that have kept you from living your dreams and being exactly who you are meant to be. It is my desire to help broaden your understanding of how mental, emotional, spiritual, and even physical cleansing is extremely essential to your expansion and achievement. In this effort of fulfilling my desire, I am committed to being the midwife assigned to help you endure the labor pains of love, so that you may give birth, and breathe life into, your best self. I am here to encourage you to discover everything it takes for you to courageously and purposefully push yourself out from the inside; to stretch yourself beyond the perception of limitation and physical restraint. You will hopefully capture a greater viewpoint of how maintaining unhealthy mindsets and limiting perspectives of what has occurred, or is currently occurring in your life, affects your aspiration to be more of who you really are in each subsequent moment. By the end of this series you will comprehend how being unaware or unconscious of how you "show up" to, as well as depart from, people, situations, and circumstances contributes greatly to the lack of achievement you may be experiencing in your life.

Before we cover the "how's" of *letting go of your buts* that commonly include time management, goal setting, modifying environments, and building healthy relationships (all of which will be covered in later volumes of LGOYB), I am opting to take a little more personal approach to self-actualization. Thus, our collective desire to experience more love, fulfillment, gratification, and achievement will be nurtured in an iterative fashion. This way we can to delve well beneath the layers of wounds, doubts, and fears that have suppressed our potential until now.

Ever heard the saying, "You don't have to eat the whole elephant…?" Well, it is my belief that before we can develop the practice of modifying our behaviors that dissuade progress and success, we must first understand why we developed poor habits in the first place. We need to get to the root cause of why we lost inspiration, why we developed low self-esteem, why we have poor time management, or why we start projects and never seem to finish them. We need to figure out what it is within that keeps us from stretching ourselves beyond physical limitation, keeps us apprehensive, keeps us scared, or keeps us playing it safe whenever faced with the need for truth-telling, adjustments in our behaviors, or a shift in perspective and outlook. We need to figure out why we feel so inclined to continue living small rather than allowing our lights to shine bright enough to inspire others to do the same. We need to figure out when we stopped loving ourselves and why. And lastly, we need to learn how to start loving ourselves again, fully and unapologetically.

Love (my reference to Spirit, Universe or the God of your own understanding) is no respecter of person when it comes to the responsibility of fulfilling a respective purpose with which we all have been tasked. As I open myself up to the process of learning and growing, I realize I will never arrive to a place of completion or all-knowingness. I have come to understand that I am constantly arriving to new opportunities for growth daily. I know, now, that the moment I consider myself to have arrived at a certain level thinking and being, is the exact day I stop living. *Let Go of Your But!* exemplifies this lesson. As I mentioned earlier, in each moment I thought I "knew enough," something else would arise to teach me otherwise. Wisdom has also helped me understand the power that comes with my choice to depart from experiences and circumstances – no matter how painful and pleasant – with the awareness that they arose to teach me exactly what I needed for a later experience.

This series is a testament to the decision to be obedient to my purpose and stay the course – *no matter what*. It hasn't always been easy. I humbly admit that there have been several days, weeks, and even months where I have entertained my own excuses. Many of them I have been able to overcome, however, there are some that continue to be *thorns in my side*, especially the older I have grown. I have awakened on many days to find myself silently proclaiming, *"I would love to finish this book...but I can't seem to find the time to complete it...but I am just too busy."* There have been many a night I spent lying awake in bed, begging for God to show me the way to balance the busy-ness of my life, so that I may find just a few moments to work on "my purpose."

Imagine the tragedy of me allowing *the perception* (let's face it...that's all it really is) of not having enough time to become a reality. Envision this possibility from two different aspects: me as the author and you as the reader. As an author, the reality of this statement would mean I forfeited the opportunity to teach, and then share, what I needed to learn; to be used as a faucet through which inspiration and insight could flow. As a reader, the reality of this statement would mean I selfishly forfeited your opportunity to receive *exactly* what you need to spark forward movement in your life; to reach your full potential; to becoming exactly who you are destined to become. There is an abundance of possibilities that may have been relinquished had the perception of *not enough time* been made into a reality I maintained. However, I will assume you get the gist of the message I am attempting to convey.

If you are reading or listening to this book, it is very likely that something within you was ignited as your eyes skimmed across its cover. I would even bet there is something relatable, or even familiar behind the context of the title. How often have you entertained excuses like: *I would like to go back to school, but…I want a new job, but…I want to learn how to play the piano, but…I deserve to be in a more loving relationship, but…but…but…*There is obviously a *but* in your own life that is currently threatening to keep you from something you truly desire.

When we as women make it up in our minds to attain a goal, arrive to a place, or accomplish a dream, many of us face a level of apprehension or anxiety that often derails us from the path to fruition. We can witness this via our choices and decisions – or lack thereof – we make when attempting to balance the energy we invest in our careers, relationships, families, businesses, etc. We don't necessarily differ from men as it relates to the tendency to make excuses and justifications about why we fall short of completion. However, the *reasons* we allow excuses to *hinder us from progressing* in our quest to be and experience more of who really are vary significantly. I know plenty of men who make excuses for not reaching their potential. Yet, much of *our* inability to rise above unwanted circumstances, or even to realize some of our deepest aspirations, has plenty to do with our propensity to neglect ourselves, or even harbor a sense of "not enough-ness" or unworthiness when we contemplate all of the things that appears to be lacking in our lives.

Many of us are unaware of what we are truly saying to ourselves, and the world at large when we allow ourselves to express excuses and justifications that impede our path to progress, and are prompted by our emotions surrounding past experiences or faulty perspectives of our circumstances. Here is an example:

> To say, "I would love to complete this book, *but* I can't seem to find the time" is to also say, "I truly see the value in writing this book, but I am unworthy of allowing myself to *make* the time I need to complete it. I am also not willing to do what I need to do in order to complete this book so that *others* in the world may be inspired."

In this scenario, the appearance of not enough time supersedes the *intention to love myself enough* to reach full potential, as well as surrender to the purpose of *offering myself as love* to the world as inspiration by way of my writing. This is an unconscious choice to neglect the call to be, and contribute to, something greater than myself. Inadvertently, I wind up subscribing to this false notion that says, "I would prefer to live small and allow work, friends, television, partying, etc. to be more valuable than my potential legacy." For some, that is okay. It is relative to each individual. However, I am inclined to believe that we all have a reason for "being here," as well as something significant to leave behind in the process. Each of us deserves to fulfill our respective vision and purpose.

The impression of unworthiness derived from cultural and societal conditioning is sometimes deeper than we can out rightly conceive. Historically, there are reasons why our – women in general – path to progress has been more challenging than those pursued by our counterparts. Playing it safe, not rocking the boat, keeping our heads down, putting children before our careers and unsuccessfully balancing professional objectives against personal passions has made it easy for us to be dissuaded from the success we desire. I would be the first to challenge the perception that women are incapable of reaching high levels of achievement. Nor could I agree with the idea that implies the level of a woman's confidence tends to be lower than men as a result of incompetence. Truthfully, many of us are guilty of selling ourselves short in lending our talents, expertise, and experience consequent to how we are perceived and accepted in this society.

Yes, it is apparent that we have advanced when we compare the number opportunities awarded to women today versus those granted during the 40's and 50's, or even earlier. Several research studies carried out around the globe indicate that organizations are now employing women by the groves; that companies who elect to hire women in larger numbers gain a greater sense of profitability and increase the chances of performing at higher levels than their competitors. Thus, it is safe to say that times are definitely changing. As we begin to capitalize on the evolution of our fate as women, we can now be a little more accountable for the inability to harmonize our lives. We can now begin to weigh the costs of failing to overcome the challenges that prohibit us from creating what we desire most. We can pursue our dreams even when we are uncertain of how to do so as a single parent. We can raise the bar of evolution and success *while* we raise our children. We can make better relationship choices now that we are no longer fully dependent upon another to feed, clothe, and provide a home for us, as well as our children. We can make better decisions about the company we keep, and weed out unnecessary relationships that do nothing but deplete time, space, emotion and energy from our lives. We can develop our inner landscapes and live as the highest versions of ourselves, in spite of unpleasant circumstances. We can do the work it takes to lose weight, finish school, pursue a career path that is more likely to harness our goals, gifts and talents, buy a new house, earn more money, sing, dance, start a business, or…anything we aspire.

How can we do this?

It starts first with understanding *the why's* that exist beneath what appears to be missing or lacking in our lives, our outlook, our hearts, our minds and our spirits. The *Let Go of Your But!* series doesn't just support the mental journey back to our potential and beyond. This series also entails an emotional and spiritual quest inward that will hopefully teach us to be more aware of where and when we betray ourselves – even if done inadvertently. It's about seeing where we have been dishonest about who we really are or what we truly desire. My hope is that we are able to recognize when and where we began to distrust the potential for reaching our highest aspirations. The aim is to help us uncover the moments where we have devalued ourselves for the sake of loving and building others up. Increasing awareness about where we are selling ourselves short, or neglecting to be authentic in our relationships, finances, spiritual lives, or our educational (traditional and nontraditional) and professional endeavors is now paramount. To evolve, we must expose the hidden moments in our past where we twiddled our thumbs in anticipation, waiting for permission to rise up and get what we want out of life. The time has come for us to make healthier choices that support our highest form of well-being. It's time we go completely "out of our minds" in order to lead lives void of limitation.

The time has come to lean on the progress and triumph of our foremothers. It's time to recognize the lessons we have acquired thus far in our own respective journeys. It's time to understand the resolve of utilizing what may have been experienced as pain and discomfort as foundations for wisdom. *Let Go of Your But!* is an urgent call to action for women who are willing to be accountable and no longer allow themselves to be the root cause to their sense of inadequacy. Let's agree to make an attempt to lovingly shed light on our collective path to creativity, potential and possibility. The desire to overcome the excuses that prohibit success and fulfillment is not about winning, losing or gaining a competitive advantage over one another – or anyone for that matter. It's about recognizing that if we were to answer the call to action to be our best selves – individually, and even more powerfully, as a collective – the need for competition would be replaced by love and acceptance. And yes, it's about realizing how victory will continue to manifest as long as we *decide* to overcome, to prevail and to take the first step…and the next…and the next, even in the face of fear and reservation.

I chose the approach of an inclusive journey with you as an attempt to participate in the collective endeavor of evolution we will make as women. The inference behind my decision involves the aspiration to promote healing on a large scale. To contribute toward the healing of *one* woman at a time creates a ripple effect of restoration that will expand to reach all women; to heal many women is to create the epicenter of change of which the world is in need.

No offense, Ladies, *but* the time has come for us to own who we are from the inside out. That means we have to recognize that we are more than our problems, more than our past, more than our shortcomings, and certainly more than our current circumstances. As divine expressions of love in its highest form, we are sisters, mothers, grandmothers, aunts, and friends. We are confidants, lovers, and nurturers blessed with the same strength, power, wisdom, compassion, and genius possessed by our Creator. As the ultimate "bringers of life," it's time we *know* that we are worthy of everything we desire to be, have, create, and experience. As we elevate ourselves in love and embrace the role of being "our sister's keeper," we hold the responsibility of lifting one another up as we amble along the shores of possibility. Learning to trust and rely on this power, this wonderful gift of creation and invigoration, is essential to our obligation to not only *live*, but to *thrive*. The world requires us to contribute to a call for restoration and wellbeing that is much bigger than our individual selves.

As we make the decision to discover our own potential and traverse our assigned journeys with purpose and intention, we must also trust that God will conspire. At the same time, it is imperative that we opt to serve as reliable sources of inspiration to one another and no longer tolerate being held back by our fears, disadvantages, or limitations. The choice to *let go of our buts* is our response to this urgent call to action in such a time as this – politically, socially, and culturally.

So, whether you are a woman who "has it all together" and yet has found yourself in need of "something different," or you are a woman in need of a healing or breakthrough, the *Let Go of Your But!* series is for you. I encourage you to grab a pen, a journal, and a box of tissues in preparation for a journey toward change.

WARNING: Should you opt to continue reading, you will be forever charged with being accountable, letting go of your excuses, unleashing your fears, embracing new possibilities, and continuously cultivating your mind to gain a level of clarity that will enable you to choose in accordance to loving yourself *truly*. Now…let's welcome the changes that are about to take place in your life, and in the world, consequent to your choice to release the *buts*.

Volume 1
Self-Love

What Really Matters...
A Story of Inspiration

"Only as high as I reach can I grow. Only as far as I seek can I go. Only as deep as I look can I see. Only as much as I dream can I be."
- Karen Ravn

There are several events throughout our lives that cause us to encounter and transcend various stages of our evolution as women. Some are painful, while others serve to be fruitful and enlightening. Some are filled with joy, pleasure, and laughter; while others may be difficult, yet somehow prompt us to make monumental shifts in our awareness and our sense of being. There are very few moments, however, that encompass all four of the elements listed above at one time. Today, I am fortunate to say that I have encountered such an experience. As much as it pains me to share this occurrence, it is my intention to show how life-altering experiences can be used to move mountains in our journeys towards success, fulfillment, or happiness.

A few years ago, a very close and dear friend of mine was diagnosed with a life-threatening disease a mere eight months prior to her passing. It was as her health began rapidly deteriorating that I felt inclined to journal my experience so that I may always remember the impact of the lesson learned. I will be vulnerably honest in saying that watching her transition from a healthy, independent, and vibrant individual to a frail, reliant, and lifeless being tore my heart into a million pieces. However, as incredibly difficult as this period of my own life may have been, I could never clear my heart of the empathy I held for her demise. To do otherwise by considering my pain felt extremely selfish. Wasn't she the one suffering? I ached terribly; however, there was no way I could allow myself to be wrapped up in my own emotions. It wasn't easy; but setting aside my own self-regarding feelings for the sake of holding her hand through the various stages of her illness was comforting to both of us. The thought of her suffering through this phase in her life without me being physically, mentally, emotionally, and spiritually present was not something I could have lived with. The comprehension that her life would soon come to an end is what kept me in the front row, applauding and encouraging the best performance in the final act of her years on earth. And though I hated to see her suffer, I am so very grateful for the time we spent together – even up to the day she passed away. In the end, the truth of the matter is that her eight-month battle was, at the time, the most exhausting, sorrowful, and most arduous occurrence I'd ever endured in all of my years.

    As to be expected, memories of those days are both filled with agony and joy, especially now that she is no longer in physical form. However, it is not her passing that saddens me most when it comes to accepting her physical absence. The lessons I learned about life at the expense of hers, came through watching how she conducted herself throughout this trial. In part, it was a beautiful sight to see how much she was loved, as friends from all over the country put forth great effort into "letting her see her flowers" before her time here on Earth came to an end. As a loving mother, daughter, sister, and wife, she'd managed to unknowingly impact hundreds of people's lives, just by being herself – funny, vivacious, caring, and loving. Words cannot express the gratitude I feel in knowing that God allowed her to see just how much she meant to people before she said goodbye.

There is another side to this story that I must share with the sole purpose of portraying the full gist of why and how much this encounter has affected me. It is however the very spark that led me to write this series. This experience serves as the hidden force that pushed me to inscribe this powerful message so that others may also be inspired to make appropriate, healthy, and constructive choices and decisions in their own lives. I feel compelled to state first and foremost that the following memories are not the *only* ones I have of my Dear Sister in Spirit. There are many that are extremely influential and enlightening. We shared many great times filled with fun and laughter and all the ups and downs that best friends bear together. The reminiscences of our friendship will be treasured forever. I am merely using the accounts that I am about to disclose as an example of how and why we as women should choose to live the greatest lives our imaginations can conceive. And, we should choose to live them NOW. I am certain the sharing of this account will encourage you in the same way it consistently restores my faith whenever I am reminded. Because I know that millions of women around the world stay in situations that may be unhealthy, I offer these words with intentions to enthuse, rather than place judgment.

Though I wish this were not the case, what most people did not know about my friend was that well beneath the façade that "everything was fine in her world," lived an extremely unhappy and lonely person. Sure, she had her children, loving sisters, brothers, and mother. She had the nice house in the suburb with two cars parked in the driveway and a lucrative job at a prominent Fortune 500 company. Underneath her loving exterior was a woman who'd been striving to find a way to pursue a level of happiness that existed outside of her immediate world. Why was this the case? The truth is, my dear friend had been in a conflicted marriage for the remaining twelve years of her life.

In her defense, she'd made several attempts to prevent discontent from extinguishing her dreams, one of which entailed becoming a celebrity photographer. But it was the burdensome distraction of despair that kept her from realizing her aspirations and loving herself to full potential. The harsh reality is that she'd spent much of those twelve years waiting for the *right* time to save money for a divorce. She deliberated over finding the *right* time and the *right* amount of money that would enable her to rent or purchase a home of her own that would accommodate three growing boys. Her thinking was that when this happened, she'd then be able to invest the *right* amount of time and energy into her aspirations of becoming an entrepreneur. Another justification she maintained for living such a stagnant existence was the idea that people would think negatively of her as a divorced, single mother. Hence the reason she spent much of her time *waiting* for her husband to leave, *waiting* for her finances to get better, *waiting* for a miracle to take place so that she could have the life she truly desired. Thus, she'd ultimately be enabled to escape her miserable existence without being perceived an unfit mother to her children for breaking up the family. It is safe to conclude that she never quite understood how waiting merely sanctioned her need to carry out the façade and nothing more. In the end, the time she lost was a heavy price to pay for the sake of an image.

Finally, one year prior to her illness, my beloved friend managed to muster up the ambition to learn the business of photography. Wisely, she decided to use this knowledge to raise the money she needed to meet her goals and live the life she'd desired to live for quite some time. After forty-seven years, she was finally beginning to take the steps necessary to move – outward, onward, and upward. I couldn't have been more proud or happier for her. Unfortunately, two days before she was to divorce herself from her husband, she received some rather difficult news. As a result of the stress caused by a failing marriage, of tension and toxins that had been poisoning her home environment, and of the grief that had held her hostage for far too long, my friend was informed that she had stage four pancreatic cancer.

I am sure you can fathom the anger she may have felt about being robbed of her chance to be happy. At least, this was her initial reaction. Because of her disappointment, she gave up on life at the moment of diagnosis. One would imagine that she would use the anger as fuel to fight for life, to fight to live happily for the remainder of her days, to live and fulfill all of the dreams that had been nestled in her heart for the better part of her healthy years. As her biggest cheerleader, I tried my damndest to encourage my friend to go on trips, to go for walks, and to appreciate the life she had left. I tried my best to push her to do the *little things* that made life matter when she was healthy. Yet, bitterness caused her to shut down. I regretfully say that the only time she left the house was to receive her treatments and attend her weekly checkups. Seldom did she leave the confines of her home to engage in activities that would arouse joy, gratitude, or self-love. There was no shopping, no photography adventures, no trips, no visits. She did nothing that would make her happy.

Until that point, I'd never witnessed anything so sad and disheartening.

Her reasoning:

> I must get my rest. If I rest, then I could get healthy. When I am healthy, I can have lunch with my friends, go to a beach, or go for a drive to the park with my boys.

Again, she was waiting for the right time. She lived – or neglected to live – those eight months relying on whatever hope she could maintain, waiting to hear the doctor say, "You are healed. You can have your life back now." That day never came. Needless to say, I can only imagine there to be more regret, anger, and disappointment in her heart when the doctor informed her that she would not survive her battle.

Luckily, this angel had made an impact on so many people – friends and family – throughout her life. For we were the ones who visited her, brought her gifts, made her laugh and smile. We tried our very best to pick her up when she no longer had the strength to carry on. Now in the memory of her last smiles, her last laughs, and even her last days, I still wish she'd chosen differently, to fight harder and to smile wider. Yet, I realize, that was *my* desire, not hers. Eventually, I came to accept that this was her process and not my own. I had to finally accept that each person responds to life's trials differently. One of the hardest things I've ever had to do was remain conscious of my emotions throughout and after this ordeal. For years, I fought hard not to grow angry as result of my own concept of survival. Still to this day, tears fill my eyes as I struggle with trying to understand why she neglected to choose to do things that would make her last moments unforgettable. I fail to understand why no amount of begging changed her mind then, and it could not change things when she eventually took her last breath. Yet still, through the sadness, I am at least inspired by the visions of the several hundred people who flocked to her funeral to celebrate her life.

People make choices. We don't always understand them. We don't always know what is going on inside as a result of what occurs behind the closed doors of their homes, or in their most significant relationships. We most certainly do not know how we would act if we found ourselves in life-altering predicaments. But what we can do, Ladies, is try to make best of the life we *do* have *now*, so that time is not lost or wasted.

It is because of this encounter with death – or life, depending on perspective – that I feel compelled to move gently into this segment of my evolution of self. It was one thing to walk away from the experience fueled by all the gifts and clarifications that come with loss, all of which ultimately helped me to understand the concept and the power of *now*. Yet it would have been another thing to walk the face of this Earth hoarding all that I'd been enlightened enough to ascertain consequent to this account. How could I keep this to myself? What good would it do? After the funeral, after all the empathy and sympathy granted to me by friends and loved ones subsided, I was left alone to deal with my newly changed reality. There I was, drowning in sorrow, standing on the edge of a cliff, on the brink of allowing pain to consume me. If I was going to turn this experience into something constructive, I was going to have to make some profound decisions in my life. If you have ever dealt with the loss of a loved one – and this was my first time – you can relate to the battle of fighting the urge to succumb to the sadness derived from the thought of moving on without them. I had no idea how I was going to do so, especially with a big, gaping wound on my heart.

An interesting thing happened to me the day after my friend's memorial. I was listening to a speaker talk about the instances in her life that catapulted her into change, going from depressed drug addict to a successful author. She shared with us listeners how the life-altering moment of enlightenment in her life came the day she lost her mother. It was during that timely interview that I heard her share the following message: "We as humans tend to feel pain and suffering when we see our loved ones go. We cry at their memories or whenever we feel their absence. Thus, we internalize what we are feeling in those instances and attribute it to pain; it is through this perception of pain that we suffer from loss. When my mother took her last breath, I chose not to suffer. To do this, I had to change my outlook. As I saw my mother lying there, staring into her eyes, silently realizing that her soul had made its departure, I could not stand to feel pain. Instead, I decided to perceive those moments of pain differently than I normally would have. I turned what felt like loss into feelings of love."

The author changed the paradigm of her experiences and instead of feeling excruciating grief, she taught herself to feel love and appreciation for having had the chance to share a portion of her life with her mother. Naturally, I was inspired to do the same thing as it pertained to sharing a portion of my life with Kim. Once my grieving subsided, I decided to turn my pain into love and to use it as fuel to become more purposeful in my life. I vowed that I would use the inspiration of my friend's life story to reach out to people around the world, so that they too could be enlightened and inspired to take control of their own lives in the now.

Initially, I had mixed feelings about my friend's departure. I was angry, confused, hurt, sad, happy (that she was no longer suffering), afraid (living life without my friend seemed so foreign), and at times, lost. However, as I began to contemplate the author's words, I found myself discovering a sense of joy. I began to accept that God knew what he was doing all along when He made our – my friend and me – paths cross. *My purpose* for being a part of her life was to contribute to the many smiles she had throughout our friendship, especially in her last days. *Her purpose* was to share her experience (death) with me so that I would be pushed and empowered to follow my dreams. Through her transition, I was reminded to avoid making the same mistakes she'd made. It was through this life changing experience that I am able to understand and grasp the concept that not a single one of us can be considered failures as long as we refuse to leave this life without achieving our dreams, goals, and aspirations. For that I am truly grateful. I may not achieve every one of my goals that I've set for myself going forward, *but* you can best believe I am going to try my best.

"The pursuit of happiness" is a well-known cliché that is used quite often in parables or tales of inspiration. In fact, I used it once or twice in this book as a means of getting you to align yourself with the start of your journey towards success and fulfillment. The truth of the matter, My Friend, is that there is no such thing as a pursuit of happiness and love. If I learned anything from my friend's passing, I learned that happiness is either in you or it isn't. So, here is another important lesson: *your road to the experience of love and happiness should be a rather short one.* All you have to do is look within. Inside of you is where you will find all you need to make self-actualization a possibility. Now, hopefully you can see why putting off something you desire – whether it is starting a family, taking a cooking class, or building a business from the ground up – is detrimental to the fruition of your potential and your entire existence. Turning within to "pursue happiness and love" is worth every bit of effort it will take to help you realize your intended self. In this now moment, I urge you to choose *you*, the real you, over your excuses. You are truly worth it.

Understanding Your "Why?"

"The journey of 1,000 miles begins with one first step."

- Lao Tzu

I'd like to share a few intimate thoughts with you in hopes of inciting you to open your eyes, ears, mind, heart and spirit in preparation for all that you are about to learn throughout this short, yet, significant time that we will share together.

A few years ago, I was speaking with a dear friend of mine – a loyal and kindhearted friend who believes in being honest to the umpteenth degree. Through this conversation, I was made aware of my propensity to use the conjunction "but" during our exchanges. I can assume that if I used "but" during our conversations, I most likely used "but" in *all* of my conversations, including those I held with myself. Instinctively, I grew defensive, especially as thoughts of my elementary school days began to flash before me. I remember so well how my fourth grade teacher, Ms. Miller, often scolded her young students for using "but" or "I can't" whenever we were selected to answer a problem or resolve a classroom matter. To say the least, I found myself standing in front of my friend horrified by the limited portrayal of me I was unconsciously and habitually presenting.

In my mind, I was an overtly decisive and optimistic person. The people closest to me at the time would have also added that I was extremely conscious, deliberate, wise, and enlightened beyond my years. True, I had my challenges at the times, several in fact, *but* I'd also accrued some monumental accomplishments over the recent years; at least enough to eradicate any perceptions of being an underachiever.

Apparently, I was wrong!

Suddenly, the thought of using "buts" in my conversations seemed so appalling, atrocious even. As far as I was concerned, I'd achieved so much in my life already, with plenty more aspirations to conquer in the near horizon, so how was it possible that I'd grown accustomed to spewing such limiting dialog? I'd traveled across country, produced television shows, written books and plenty of articles, started my own online publishing company, and used my artistic skills to create greeting cards and athletic apparel. I'd hosted a couple of radio programs and even started a few businesses, most of them unsuccessful, but that is beside the point. Needless to say, I was completely oblivious as to how such a single word had infiltrated what I thought was an impeccable, accomplished vocabulary.

I finally found the courage to stop running from this horror and confront myself in the mirror. After several moments of silence, one glaring question rang loudly throughout my mind: *Even with everything I'd achieved or accomplished thus far, had I come close to attaining the level of success that was in alignment with my true potential?*

I waited patiently for the candor of my spirit, certain that I'd soon hear an emphatic *"yes!"* Yet it was a few short moments later when I finally responded with a resounding *"no."*

From that moment forward, I began listening to myself whenever I spoke. I was quite shocked to discover that my noble friend had been right. "Buts" decorated my internal and external conversations like tiny sparkling Christmas tree ornaments. Recognizing the possibility that I had become my very own obstacle to reaching full potential was horrifying. There had already been so many hurdles that I had been fortunate enough to surmount or circumvent in my journey. Never once had I considered myself to be an impediment of any kind. True, there were so many endeavors and ambitions that resided in my heart, but I figured I would get to them eventually, just as I'd done with everything else. It had yet to cross my mind that putting them off until later was much like allowing pieces of myself to sit in desolate corners of an abandoned house, without food or nutrition. Having the routine usage of the word "but" brought to my attention helped me to understand why certain levels of success for which I aspired had yet to be carried out in my physical existence. It took an embarrassing moment for me to truly understand the impact of what a single word had on my life. It was also that same moment that revealed to me just how unloving it would be for me to continue using it. As far as I was concerned, negating my potential was completely unacceptable behavior.

The irony to this awakening was the flashing memory of a former colleague explaining her perspective of a "but." She'd stated that "a 'but' negates everything that comes before it." Now having a reference of my own to which I could apply such prudence, I was able to comprehend that anything I claimed I wanted to achieve would dissipate the moment the word "but" came out of my mouth. Normally, whenever I heard the word "but" I automatically thought of the hunk of meat sitting on my backside that followed me everywhere I went. Only my "buts" were far from synonymous with the word *behind*. They actually served as barriers standing *before* me.

After taking the time to analyze the gap between my current self and the self I envisioned becoming. I realized that I'd actually traveled very little distance on the path to success I'd mapped out in years prior. Deep down I knew I was meant for greatness, but I didn't understand why, after placing significant amounts of effort toward projects and ventures, I was not getting any closer to fulfilling my truest intentions for success. Suddenly it dawned on me: *It's possible that I would have been much further in my dreams had I not been tiptoeing across pathways and shortcuts cluttered with "buts."*

What this brought home for me was the fact that the power of a "but" is actually more commanding than the intention preceding its expression. As much as it pained me to hear and accept such a revelation, it was exactly what I needed to help shed light on the aspects of my life that required change. Truthfully, I wish I'd had this information much sooner. Though, I still argue that I would have been so much further along in my stream of accomplishments had the truth been revealed to me sooner than later, I am also able to distinguish the difference between failure and delayed learning. As the saying I mentioned earlier goes: "When the student is ready the master appears." Thus, I can now relish in the beauty of finally arriving to the moment of receiving what I needed to know in order for me to *do* better and *be* greater.

All in all, I learned the lesson, made the necessary adjustments, and adhered to the process of evolution and self-awareness. My story demonstrates how it wasn't until I was *ready* to receive such a poignant message that I could be made aware of the mistakes I'd been making. As a result, I was able to witness what happens when I choose to be still and listen. I was able to recognize my soul's yearning to experience more of myself and release the inclination to make excuses for my limitations and deficiencies.

I accept that there are still so many other things I need to learn in preparation for the greatness I envision; however, I am truly grateful for the lesson I shared above. I know of the potential within me that will one day soon be realized as long as I consciously move forward without imposition. I suppose the greatest take-away from that enlightening experience was the notion of how having a limited understanding and a skewed vision of possibility, purpose, and passion had a great impact on my ability to recognize my full potential. Lack of self-love, as well the wherewithal to speak outwardly and constructively about my aspirations made it impossible for me to create the experience of fruition in my life. The more aware I became of the limiting conversations I had with myself and others, not to mention the continuous negation of what I truly desired, the more I began to recognize how a change in mindset would significantly alter the outcome and direction of my quest for achievement and fulfillment. Needless to say, and as you will read later on in this book, mastering the ability to generate self-love, maintain unwavering belief in my ability, and realize my aspirations at full capacity did not happen immediately or overnight. It took a great deal of patience and practice, which was not always easy.

♥♥♥♥♥

Self-love, passion, and purpose are all vital components in our pursuit of happiness, success, fulfillment, achievement, and freedom in life. The potential for reaching our goals and ambitions rests on our ability to cultivate these intrinsic aspects of our existence. Reaching full potential is also contingent upon us discovering meaning for our lives, or at the very least, having a purpose that supports every action, choice or decision we make. These shifts will in turn feed our hunger to find meaning to all of our ideas and true desires. They will move us to expand our awareness of why we justify our shortcomings and limitations rather than overcome them. We make ourselves susceptible to experiencing overwhelming amounts of fear, destruction, sabotage, and harm when we fail to at least attempt discovering why we are here in this world. Without passion, purpose, and self-love, we are completely incapable of consciously choosing and standing in our power (being fully aware of and owning who we are truly) to create exactly what we desire to have, be, or experience. Our actions and outcomes are all derive from our ability to tap into both our individual, as well as collective power. The quest of exploring the deeper parts of ourselves where meaning resides is what makes the pain, the agony, the fight, and the suffering we endure worthwhile. It's what drives us to delve into our ambitions, and fuels the innate desire within to evolve, expand, and excel.

    Self-love serves as an internal guidance that directs us to choose and ultimately decide in ways that support good health and well-being. Practicing self-love is not to be confused with "loving ourselves" narcissistically. To choose to love from this perspective will only lead us to become our own object of love, distracting us from our primary purpose for existing - sharing love and being of service to others. Self-love in this context is more about the awareness, attainment, and expansion of peace, freedom, compassion, and authentic expression of our true potential. Self-love prompts us to refrain from rejecting ourselves, as well as our feelings, as we embark upon a path to experience more of who we really are on the inside. As a collective, we as women find it challenging to overcome unhealthy thoughts and beliefs that exist consequent to comparing ourselves, our choices, and our successes to those made by our friends, peers, family, and significant others. We continuously make the painful mistake of scrutinizing our bodies and measuring them against imagery shared in media. Because many of us lack self-love, we are quick to give away our power of choice to people, environments, and circumstances that are utterly undeserving and unworthy. It is through our willingness to love ourselves *first*, in spite of past mistakes and failures, and without judgment, shame, guilt, or regret, that we will recognize that there are no "wrong" roads. Each past and present road we elected to travel have led us exactly where we are in this moment. There are no wrong choices. All of the events that have led us to the current moment, the here and now, were essentially presented to us as opportunities to make a brand-new choice that will send us traipsing down a brand-new road.

Purpose provides us with the "why" behind our choice to explore, as well as our decision to endure challenges throughout our lives. I've learned that life isn't so much about the "what" or the "how" of your greatest dreams and aspirations, as it is about the "whys" that support them. Embracing or developing the purpose of our lives will essentially give us a greater sense of meaning. Meaning then becomes the driving force that compels us to stretch beyond limitations, take risks, overcome fears, and go beyond personal needs in order to positively contribute to the lives of others around us. Purpose inspires us to make a difference in the world and to fearlessly stand up for what we believe.

Passion incites us to go above and beyond perceived limitations with energy, enthusiasm, and excitement. In other words, our passion is the stream of ambition that, when allowed to flow, materializes into the type of action that perpetuates possibility. When coupled with purpose and self-love, passion ignites within ourselves the capacity to create change in our lives, and more importantly, in the lives of those who surround us. Embarking upon a life that is directly aligned with our purpose helps us to differentiate *true* goals, desires, and ideas of success and fulfillment from those that stem from the wants and desires of our peers, parents, and media. Regardless of our current job, circumstance, relationship, business venture, performance goal, or a lifelong dream, identifying our passion and aligning it with truth, purpose, and an optimistic attitude is the foundation for success. Passion is what makes us unafraid to declare something (a goal, resource, job, relationship, house, etc.) as already existing, and then act on that inner declaration until the aspiration has been realized.

Creating a life to which we aspire not only takes work, but it also takes a higher level of diligence to bring forth into physical reality what we envision in our dreams. Having an increased awareness of the need for changes or shifts in mindsets is the beginning of a noteworthy process of evolution that most people are either unwilling or incapable of undergoing. To maintain momentum towards the desired intentions, turning our thoughts into actions must also become a daily practice. Though not always easy to accomplish when things fail to transpire as planned or hoped, it's imperative that we refrain from focusing on thoughts and perceptions that invoke depression, discontent, disappointment, and discouragement. We must be quick to remember that *nothing* stays the same and that all conditions and circumstances are temporary. Therefore, optimism and open mindedness goes a long way in respect to how we go about the pursuit of happiness and fulfillment. As our outlook begins to expand, we will begin to recognize how opportunities to make new choices and decisions seem to appear more frequently. Hindsight will reveal how the opportunities were always available, yet our awareness simply required stretching for them to be perceived. The words of Dr. Wayne Dyer explain it best through this statement: *Change how you look at things and the things you look at will change.*

As a woman with a great amount of compassion, I can relate to how easy it is to get caught up in our emotions about what is or is not occurring and waiting for things around us to change. We all have (at some point in our lives) been guilty of "practicing patience" or "having faith" as we waited hopelessly for the people, things, dreams, and experiences we desired to show up in our lives exactly as we envision. It's easy for us to become so engrossed in our emotions that we neglect to carry out the task of staying focused on possibility, investing in our wellbeing and trying to positively alter our perception of the things that are showing up in our lives. We miss the mark when it comes to being responsible and observing how all experiences and circumstances arise, consequent to how we view our potential and ourselves.

The attainment of everything we aspire to have, be, or experience begins from within, rather than from the outside. All this means is that we must recognize our power and ability to become an intrinsic part of the solutions we seek, rather than being, or contributing to, the problems that stand before us. It means that we must learn to shift our focus of attention from what no longer works and on to what we love about ourselves, our lives, our circumstances, and our relationships. Therefore, polishing up our emotional, mental, and spiritual well-being until gratitude and appreciation can once again radiate from our hearts is of the essence.

Again, realizing we may be stuck in a state of what may seem to be "changelessness" is a great accomplishment. In the well-known inspirational movie, *The Secret*, Dr. Joe Vitale says, "…a lot of people feel stuck, confined, or imprisoned by their current circumstances…whatever your circumstances are right now, understand that is only your current reality." Our current reality begins to change the moment we invest time into changing perceptions, expectations, actions, degrees of focus, and words spoken out of our mouth. To change our circumstances, we must first change our thinking. Vitale goes on to say, "Most people look at their current state of affairs and say 'this is who I am.' It's not who you are, it's who you were. Your current state of affairs are the residuals of your past thoughts and actions." Such a powerful statement, wouldn't you agree? With this awareness, we can begin to consider our thoughts, perceptions, and beliefs as investments we are making toward our future. It's enough to motivate us to make a monumental shift in how we are thinking, believing, speaking, and choosing in and about our current state of existence.

There are plenty of people in this world who remain bound by misery and failure, feeling as though they are without chance for escape, simply because they refuse to take inventory as to why and how their lives became sedentary in the first place. Perceived limitations are also a result of our unwillingness to be accountable for whatever is or is not occurring in our lives at any given moment. Happiness entails freedom, and the most important freedom we've inherited is the freedom of choice. Every circumstance, every relationship, every job, *everything* that has occurred, or is occurring, in our lives did so, or is doing so, as a result of a choice that was made or not made. This includes the choice to maintain specific perspectives, as well as to carry out responses (good or not so good) to situations that occurred in our past or are occurring in our present.

One of the greatest insights I would like for us to comprehend is that a life without evolution or progress is the equivalent of quitting, withdrawing or even dying. Because life itself is constantly evolving, this means that all living things are either growing and increasing toward maturity, or they are deteriorating toward decay and death. Not a single one of us is exempt from the law of nature. The greatest intention of our lives is to come forth as envisioned or intended, to explore avenues and to discover new possibilities so that we may ensure the realization of the self that resides at the very core of our being. Many of the bouts of stagnation we experience has much to do with fear or the lack of understanding. There are is also the lack of truth, will, motivation, or even the awareness required to either create something new. Stagnation and complacency occur when we impede the flow of our reason for being or lose sight of what it means to love ourselves fully, without apologies, excuses, or explanations.

Being that we are on the path of loving ourselves into full potential, which will first invoke our ability to overcome excuses, the particulars of how our circumstances came to be what they are is of no relevance *at this stage of the game*. We can return our focus to them at a later point in this series. For the duration of this book, let us agree to focus our attention on the potential "whys" behind our indecision and inertia. In this moment, what matters most is that we have arrived to a place in our lives where modification of some sort is required for us to move forward and become more of who we are on the inside. It's even more important that we begin to delve deeper beneath the layers of our behaviors, choices, and decisions to discover the root cause of our limited perspectives and patterns. It's quite possible that we have been acting, choosing, and speaking unconsciously.

The good news is that we are momentarily inspired to push ourselves over the mountain of fear and mediocrity. Now, to maintain momentum, here is what we need to know: *in order to create change in our lives, in order to move from where we are currently to our truest, most desired place in life, we must be willing to rediscover our hunger and thirst for self-realization.* The best way to achieve this is to focus all of our energy on learning how to love ourselves completely. It will also take a willingness to cultivate goodness in the most important relationship we will ever have - with ourselves.

As happy as I am that you have arrived at this point of awareness, I must warn you that after reading this book, you will no longer feel inclined to use the same excuses you have been using up until this point. Because you are on the path of cultivating self-love, you will no longer permit yourself to continue "but-ing" all over your dreams. No longer will you allow yourself to use self-limiting justifications.

The *"buts"* stop here. You are here to *love yourself into being* exactly as you envision. Now that you are on your way to *knowing* better, it's time to start *doing* better.

Standing before you is an opportunity to a make different choice and to open your eyes to the fact that excuses are merely negative conditions you've generated, recorded, and replayed over and over in your mind to justify your failure to take action. Today is a new day! On this day, you will begin to pursue your own individuality, your own beliefs, and your own concepts that are conducive to your success and wellbeing. You will be encouraged to follow your own spirit in order to fulfill everything you are meant to become through the use of your own ideas, passions, talents, and desires.

My suggestion going forward is that you learn how to focus your mind and heart on the grand possibility that exists in your tomorrow. Be certain to remain in the present moment with each step you make as you embark upon this beautiful journey of becoming. As a result, you will find that having a lack of time, being too old, not having enough resources, or your family, children, and jobs will no longer be viable obstacles that keep you from having, being, and doing exactly what you desire.

✶✶✶✶✶

There is a massive ripple that expands as each of us makes the choice to let go of the need for blame, release the pain, and embrace the lessons obtained from past mistakes. The collective energy of devotion and compassion is amplified when we begin to apply acquired enlightenment toward not just our own growth, but toward the growth of others as well. Contrarily, as long as we continue to remain disconnected from our truth, walking around with blinders covering our eyes, an obscured reality is all we can ever perceive. *Truth* and *awareness* are two significant components to the achievement of success and fulfillment in every area of our lives. Growth and transformation start from within. In order to know more of who we are, so that we may bring to fruition more of what we truly desire (collectively and individually) we must begin to ask the "right" questions beyond "why" or "why not?" Thus, I encourage you to take a moment and ask yourself the following:

- Who am I? Not who am I *currently,* but rather *who* am I *really*?

- What perceptions of myself do I hold?
    - **Tip:** Understand that the perceptions you've heard others share about you may serve as a reference point. However, try your best to dig deeper within. Go beneath the surface. Tap into the space in your heart where honesty lives to obtain a full and clear picture of what is actually being perceived.

- What honest perceptions of me do others hold?
    - **Tip:** Don't be afraid to ask those closest to you. Remember, this is for your growth. Being combative or defensive will not help. You know the truth. Just listen for what fits. Be open and accountable to receive what doesn't seem to fit as constructive feedback.

- What do I need to do to change the personal attributes I consider unfitting or displeasing?
    - **Tip:** Use the feedback you have received as well.

- Where am I in respect to where I would like to be?

- What is my truth?
    - **Tip:** Start with your dreams.

- What creative ideas have I abandoned because I was afraid of what others would think?

- Who do I need to become in order surmount the excuses that prohibit me from living my truth?

- What steps can I take to start living life as my envisioned self?

- Who do I need to become so that I may contribute to another person's growth and evolution?
    - **Tip:** If you know them, consider your talents, gifts and passions that can be used to serve others. If you are unaware of your talents, gifts, and passions, return to the question "What is my Truth?"

- What type of example would I like to be so that others are empowered and inspired to be more of who they really are?
    - **Tip:** Learn what it means to "teach what you need to know." The application of this philosophy will enable you to not only raise the bar for who you aspire to be, but it will simultaneously provide a way for you to contribute to the lives of others. Remember, the life you live is not your own. You are here to help another find their way, just as others are here to assist you along your journey. Discover ways to pay it forward.

Give yourself the time to truly hear the answers to these queries. Put the book down and allow what you hear to resonate in your spirit. Remember, there is no such thing as right or wrong answers in this scenario. There is only truth. Still, keep in mind that the truths you discover in this moment may change, evolve, weaken, or even strengthen as we continue this journey. The objective is to build a solid foundation to which you can return when you get distracted, and from where you can launch when the time comes for you to transition into your next phase of becoming more of who you really are.

The questions above are some that I asked myself once I was able to overcome the initial embarrassment derived from "but-ing" on my dreams. I wrote down my answers and pondered over them for a few days. Shortly after clearly defining the truth to these inquiries, I was able to make a calculated decision to *stop* making excuses for the part of my life that remained *unlived*. Since then, I have given my best effort to act on every single one of my aspirations – big or small. Not only have I continuously acted toward my dreams and goals, I have also put forth deliberate effort into cultivating self-love. The greater the love I have for myself, the greater I can recognize, focus on, and bring forth my true potential. The more I can recognize my true potential, the more inclined I am to allow passion to guide me into the fulfillment of my life purpose.

Tilling the Mind

"Therefore, we must fearlessly pull out of ourselves and look at and identify with our lives the living creativity some of our great-grandmothers were not allowed to know."

- Alice Walker

So many instances have arisen in my life when I felt completely confident that an *ah-ha* moment or a lesson learned was the *exact* one I needed to reach "the next level." Upon each lesson-laden encounter, I figured I would never again have to worry about running into the *same* pitfall, let alone something much worse. I, of course, have been proven wrong every single time. That is, until I grew shrewd enough to remain open to receiving a lesson or two from *everything* and *everyone* I came across in my day-to-day comings and goings. I am also able to comprehend the true essence of being humble. Never has it been clearer to me that I will never know enough, or too much about life, to be exempt from the experience of harm or pain perpetuated by mistakes and downfalls. I can only minimize the chances of falling into calamity and destruction through my willingness to expand in self-awareness. I have also learned that developing habits prompted by the need to be perfect will never make me more perfect than I already am (this was an extremely profound awareness). I will never be flawless in the eyes of anyone outside of myself, nor will I ever be absolved from making errors and oversights. Not that I was so arrogant to believe otherwise, I was just naive in thinking there would come a point where learning – or should I say accruing scrapes and bruises that come with stumbling across life's roadblocks – would stop, and the rest of my life would begin to run smoothly.

At this present moment, I can now understand that all the pain and suffering I've experienced in my life were consequent to making unconscious choices and decisions. I also know each challenging experience transpired consequent to the need to learn *exactly* what I needed in order to become *exactly* who I've aspired to be. I will be the first to attest that coming to this awareness was not so easy, nor did the pathway feel so cozy and comfortable. However, because of the work and effort I put towards understanding myself, my strengths, my gifts, and my purpose, it became easier for me to navigate through life and lessen the chance of being blindsided by whatever life reflects back to me. Thus, I can recognize and appreciate beauty in the process of growing, developing, strengthening, and improving. Because of this, I learned to seek the good, as well as the purpose, behind everyone and everything I have allowed into my life, even if it hurts.

I must humbly admit that I have had, and will most likely continue to have, many shortcomings. Perfectionism has been both a curse and a blessing in the many attempts to create my desired life. I recognize that failing or falling short of a goal and/or desired outcome, is a part of life's process. Many days passed where I felt discouraged and opted to beat myself up for getting distracted. Yet, choosing to be extremely critical of poor choices prompted by a lack of understanding is both unloving and uncompassionate.

My experiences have been kind enough to teach me how to consider the many successes I have encountered along the way, as well as recognize that the journey to fulfillment is, and will always be, one that is never ending. Thus, eliminating limiting mindsets and developing ones that promote fruition and fulfillment is a commitment I fervently strive to maintain.

Before you can understand how to let go of the "buts" that prohibit you from self-realization and triumph, I believe it is necessary to introduce some potential reasons as to why emotional, physical, spiritual, or mental impediments exist to begin with. One of them being the inability to clearly define what success means and looks like for you.

Ever heard of the adage, "you can't know where you are going until you know where you have been?" In the matter of success or achievement, to "know where you have been" means to reflect over the life you've lived thus far. In doing so, you will realize that you've lived through enough trials and tribulations to determine who, what, where, and how you would or would not like to be. In other words, you have acquired enough information by now to know what does or does not work, and what is or is not practical. To have overcome any type of adversity in life is to know that nothing is impossible. "Where you have been" is the life you have lived. "Where you are going" is the life you envision living. Use everything in between to create the path to fruition. Remember, it isn't about the destination, but rather the journey. You have everything you need to evaluate your true potential, which is most likely more than what you can possibly conceive. Instead of angrily and shamefully harping over what did not work in your past, use the contrast to first identify, and then focus upon what you need to succeed in order to experience fulfillment. Work on determining what is or is not missing and then make the necessary adjustments that enable you to surrender your excuses and move toward your intended destination or finish line.

Most books penned by specialists who advocate empowerment, self-motivation, and achievement encourage readers to tap into their inner power, fight for positioning and status, and follow a foolproof formula of execution. They promote extreme cookie cutter rules and instructions with which to live by in order to separate oneself from the norm, rise to the top, reach goals, eliminate procrastination, improve time management, overcome powerlessness, etc. Most neglect to remind their followers that measurements and definitions of success are not only relative to each individual, but that they continuously change and evolve according to where they happen to be in their respective lives. The path to success does not encompass a one-size-fits all approach.

Having studied success and leadership for over a decade, my objective is not to sell you on the idea that all things are possible through the application of hard work and dedication. For some, that is a no brainer. Understanding how to aim high, be exceptional, strive for abundance, and remain purposefully driven are all noble efforts.

However, I am not sure it is safe to assume that most people are even capable of recognizing who they need to be or become in order to begin the path to success. So, attempts to compete with the next person, dominate in one's field, and exercise power over something desired becomes futile. How can one understand what it means to be above average if there is no clear understanding of what being average entails? Or, is a person expected to know how to break through patterns of mediocrity even when creativity is rarely fostered and often discouraged? Doesn't it take a bit of imagination to even conceive of seeing, having, or being something better or greater? How can one understand what rising above normality entails when they may be completely unaware that it is even possible to be more than who they are currently? How is one able to identify areas of improvement if at first, they are not able to recognize who they are being in comparison with who they need to become to attain the success they desire? How can one understand their true potential if they aren't even cognizant of the disruptive conversations they unconsciously entertain? How is it possible for anyone to achieve any level of greatness without first recognizing the choice to love themselves fully into their true potential? These are some very profound questions that I encourage you to ponder over. Within honest deliberation in an attempt to find answers to these inquiries lies the *why* behind failed attempts to live your desired life.

Much of what I have learned by studying the works of many self-improvement, personal/professional development coaches, and following the guidance of highly admired mentors, has been extremely helpful as it pertains to developing qualities such as discipline, focus, intensified investment of time and energy, persistence, and leveraging relationships. However, at some point I had to reflect on my accomplishments, and even the aspirations I have yet to fulfill, in effort to discern whether I was living up to my full potential, or not. My honest answer was neither "yes" nor "no." At the time, I could say that I had achieved some monumental goals, and that I was still on course to reaching my full potential. But I have to admit, there have been periodic lulls and interruptions in my progress. So, the question became, "have I been able to maintain, multiply, and repeat the same formula of success *throughout all areas of my life*, as well as reach higher and greater levels of success on a continuous basis? The answer then was, "no."

I am by no means insinuating that what I learned up until that point was ineffective. After all, even though I hadn't reached levels of success to the degree in which I'd envisioned, I was nowhere near what or who I was when I started the journey. That, in itself, is commendable; however, I'd like to speak to you about success and fulfillment from a completely different perspective. Before you can endeavor the path of achievement, you must first begin to understand what obstacles lie before you. Allow me to share with you some of the practices that I have been able to maintain to help me withstand the course of achievement during tough times. I am hopeful that you, too, will be able develop these practices in order to create a life you truly desire that exists well beyond your "buts" and perceived limitations:

- Consistently check in with yourself by making honest assessments and accepting exactly where you are and who you have become thus far.

- Develop a willingness to shed light on limitations, weaknesses, and moments of betrayal (where you have been inauthentic and dishonest with yourself and others; where you have broken commitments with yourself) no matter how shameful they make you feel (remember shame and disappointment can be overcome with the right mindset and outlook).

- Remind yourself that you are either choosing or neglecting to be authentic, honest, and accountable in your relationship with yourself and with others. How and whom you choose to be within your relationships greatly impacts not just your life, but also your ability to navigate beyond the excuses, shame and perceived limitations that keep you blinded from potential and possibility. The more vulnerable and authentic you choose to be, the more possibility of creating your life as desired becomes evident.

- Identify where you have allowed or tolerated substandard behavior or treatment in your life and how it has prevented you from reaching goals and aspirations.

- Open your heart and mind to discovering how changing thoughts and perceptions of the world directly affect your ability to maintain focus when things don't go as planned.

- Regardless of what occurs around you, much of which you cannot control, remember to be patient with your emotions and prohibit them from derailing your path or clouding your vision of success and/or healing. The one thing in life that you can always control is what occurs inside of you: thoughts, perceptions, beliefs, attitude, emotions, feelings, etc.

- Use everything that occurs in your life for the betterment of yourself and your surroundings, including negative emotions that arise as a result of external conflict.

- Perceive fear as merely a state of mind designed to either promote your survival or sabotage your potential to be greater and better than you already are.

- Be at one with not only your pain, but also the collective pain of your sisters, mothers, daughters, and friends, without trying to run away from, hide, or make an immediate fix to it. The objective is not necessary to wallow in what hurts, but to simply recognize that the presence of discomfort exists for a reason. Focus energies toward healing and discovering ways with which pain can be used to strengthen your life purpose.

- Love yourself beyond the perception of judgment, limitation, or betrayal doled out by others.

- Understand that everything working or not working in your life is indicative of what is or is not occurring within you. Whatever is occurring in your life that is in complete contrast with what you prefer is emblematic of a need for healing in your beliefs, perceptions and outlook of who you really are.

- Remain utterly aware of the difference between approval and acceptance as it relates to unwise, painful, or destructive choices you have made in your past.

- Approval generates the space for conditional judgment and limitation, while acceptance generates the space for unconditional love and modification.

- You don't have to approve of where you are but accepting where you are is the only way to begin endeavoring the changes you seek in life.

- Stay in alignment with the truth that says what you experience is never about getting or not getting what you want, but always about attracting what you and who you are being from the inside.

The road we traverse during seasons of transformation is seldom painless or placid. Without the understanding of which step to take first, it is often easier for us remain defeated, stuck knee deep in the quicksand of indecision and befuddlement. However, our tendency to be overwhelmed and encumbered by the very thought of all of the things that need to take place in order to see ourselves through to the other side of our discontent can be surmounted with the right perspective, if we take the time to develop it. There are some of us who have the innate ability to confront challenges with an enthusiastic attitude that compels us to attack change head on. Others are more inclined to approach them with reluctance and disdain, not at all excited about having to move beyond their zone of comfort.

I've had the pleasure of speaking to many women who are in varying seasons in their lives, ranging from executives to athletes to high school and college graduates who have reached points in their paths where moving toward a next level or in new direction is inevitable. I've even coached women who were faced with making monumental changes in their lives ranging from marriage to divorce to bearing a child. There have also been those women who were recently diagnosed with an illness or impairment, as well as women who are about to embark upon an undertaking where the release of relationships, circumstances, and behaviors that no longer serve them is unavoidable. Out of all the different circumstances shared by the women I have encountered, the one thing that is inexplicably common among them is the sense of fear and trepidation towards the unknown into which they were about to venture. There was also the commonality of grief or loss over *what used to be* or *what could have been.*

As we transition from the old and into the new phases of our lives, it is important that we begin to decipher what of our past should be left behind and what we should take with us as we move forward, upward, and toward the preferred side of our ambition. It's important that we take responsibility of releasing certain mindsets, memories, stories, relationships, and actions that somehow hinder progress. There comes a point when the decision of letting go of the negative emotions associated with circumstances in our pasts and leaning into wisdom borne of our lessons becomes the greatest, most pivotal priority of our lives. Sometimes we neglect to understand just how crucial mental and emotional preparation is for times of transition. To empower ourselves to do the work it takes to transform into the person we need to be in order to transcend undesired circumstances is often times perceived as a fiercely ambitious undertaking. The overwhelm experienced by most when the work required for change becomes apparent is often too heavy to surmount.

This is where I make a point to remind us of the need to be compassionate and patient with ourselves as we go through the process of moving forward in spite of our fears and apprehensions. We must gift ourselves with an adjustment period that allows us to get accustomed to changes we will inevitably encounter once we make the decision to push beyond our current conditions, beliefs, and self-perceptions, as well as the environments and circumstances that no longer serve us. Though being optimistic in the face of change can seem impractical, being mentally and emotionally prepared will alleviate some of the discombobulation. This is often accomplished by sitting down and developing a plan that will enable us to take one step at a time, conquer one challenge at a time, or change one thought process at a time, rather than attempting to experience triumph and achievement in one giant step. Giving ourselves time to prepare also allows us to take things as they come day by day, rather than trying to change our thoughts, perceptions, and actions overnight.

Remember, we are in the business of loving ourselves into true potential. Therefore, we must set the stage and position ourselves to take incremental steps toward the life we desire and deserve. As we gear up to plant new seeds (thoughts, perceptions, and beliefs) we must first make sure that we have tilled and properly nurtured the soil in our garden of possibility - the mind. Another commonality experienced by women who endeavor the path of transformation is the uneasy sense that everything around us is unsettled, or in the process of shifting right before our eyes without any way to control it. To curtail this experience, it is wise to practice acknowledging that the only thing we can control in our lives is ourselves. We must also remain focused on desired outcomes, even when it appears that our world has been turned upside down.

I bring all of this up at this point in the book to prepare us for the changes that we are bound to experience in our lives as a result of choosing self-love. Because we are taking ownership of our lives and what occurs throughout, along with making new choices and decisions based on our desire to release everything that no longer adds value, we must be willing to accept that our surroundings, our relationships, our interests, our actions, and our choices are going to look different. It is through preparation that we will be empowered to cope with these modifications in a way that builds momentum toward the realization of who we really are. Change is inevitable, but we need to commit to doing whatever it takes to endure the process without breaking or folding, because to do anything less would be unloving.

The changes in life we will encounter because of choosing to love ourselves without apology won't always be pleasant. Some of them will knock us flat on our backs and leave us feeling weak and inadequate. Something else to remember along the way is that as long as we can look up, we can always get up! We can never go wrong when we opt to love ourselves first, above all else. We have to learn to trust the process, even as people, places, and things begin to look and feel different; even when the people who surround us begin to treat us different simply because we are choosing to put ourselves and our wellbeing before them. At the same time, we must be willing to acknowledge, not suppress, our affliction that is resultant of not only what we experienced in our past, but also of the upheaval that may occur consequent to what we decide to release. Such release could entail anything from a job to an emotionally burdensome relationship with a loved one to a self-sabotaging aspect of ourselves. As mentioned earlier, allowing ourselves the opportunity to grieve what was, and is no longer, or our idea of what could have been, plays a significant part in our ability to cope and move through seasons in ways that are emotionally, mentally, and physically healthy.

Two topics I would like to mention before moving on to the next chapter are *closure* and *forgiveness*. As discussed in later chapters, it is impossible to move forward in anything the future holds as long as we are still holding on to something from our past. Both our minds and hearts should remain as clear as possible for the road ahead, and not cluttered with old emotions and memories about things, people, and circumstances that no longer exist. Finding closure and forgiving ourselves, and others, for past mistakes, poor choices, and failures will enable us to move into our future unbound and enthusiastic. Closure and forgiveness surrounding relationships, jobs, decisions, and events that didn't turn out quite as planned, or expected, sheds light on the lessons that will eventually add value to our lives.

As we begin to move in the direction of our preferred state of existence, developing the ability to be authentic is extremely vital to moving beyond what did not work or serve us in the past. Therefore, allowing ourselves to grieve over the loss of, or separation from, something or someone that had a significant impact on our lives is essential. Prohibiting this process of healing will make it difficult to gather our strengths and cultivate our talents. Our ability to remain focused on the positive aspects of who we are and what we are currently experiencing would be compromised. Working to align ourselves with the support required for us to do whatever makes us feel loved and happy in life is where we should pour our energy. Thus, tilling the mind by developing new practices, behaviors, rituals, routines, and perspectives in the season of change is vital to our ability to create the life and experiences we so desire.

Beginning with Love

"Loving yourself has nothing to do with being selfish, self-centered, or self-engrossed. It means that you accept yourself for what you are. Loving yourself means that you accept responsibility for your own development, growth, and happiness. When you love yourself you pave the way for all you want and need to come to you at the right time in a perfect way."

- Iyanla Vanzant

Despite what the world may say about women who endeavor self-care through the prioritization of their needs and desires, there is a significant difference between being self-*ish* and self-*full*. You can rest assure that not one single thing which was envisioned could have come to *full* fruition without someone first having developed the ability to love themselves unashamedly and unapologetically. The energy of shame, as well as the inclination to apologize for being *exactly as we are in this* moment, impedes our ability to develop the confidence and courage required in our pursuit of achieving the *im*possible (I'm possible). True success and fulfillment are only possible once we are able to release a large amount, if not all, of the mental, emotional, and spiritual barriers that limit our potential and cloud our vision from what is truly possible in our lives. Fruition isn't solely about maintaining a vision, setting goals, and engaging in rituals that support our path to fulfillment. The one thing I fiercely believe is that self-love is the primary, most foundational piece to our ability to bring to fruition our desires and aspirations. To the degree that we experience ourselves as love is the degree in which we can tap into an innate sense of passion and purpose that compels us to thrive.

Without self-love we will often find ourselves bouncing and rolling through life like a tree with no roots, completely lost in a cyclical, bohemian existence clouded by resistance and denial. Self-love fuels our will to stand strong no matter what goes on around us, or what difficult challenges lie ahead. It enables us to consistently match the thoughts, beliefs, and choices we are required to maintain during difficulties and challenges to those we abide by when life doesn't seem so burdensome. It is what helps us to harness our power to create when everyone around us doubts our abilities. It is what compels us to decide and choose for ourselves in ways that are healthy and uplifting, affording us the opportunities to live in truth and authenticity. The absence of self-love keeps us blind from even understanding or envisioning what is truly possible for our lives and us. Without self-love, it is impossible for rituals, practices, or plans to lead us toward realizing our dreams. Sure, we will meet goals, and even create an affluent life for ourselves if we follow the carbon copy, yellow brick roads to success. Yet, it won't always mean we will experience the level of true happiness, joy, peace, and fulfillment that is abound when we are able to dig deep and love ourselves into living and being the highest possible version of who we are meant to become.

Being that women are highly emotional beings, we must learn how to use our feelings and emotions to our advantage. From this moment forward, we can strive to continuously remind ourselves of our ability to attract preferred outcomes into our lives. However, it is imperative that we are first able to intimately and authentically connect with ourselves. It is through self-connection that we can imaginatively adjoin with all that is required to bring into existence our desired experiences. To clarify, in order to allow or receive the resources, relationships, environments, circumstances, or situations required to realize a dream, we must be able to *feel* our way through the process of ushering a vision into existence. This is impractical when 1) we lack full understanding of what it means to be intimately connected and vulnerable with ourselves, 2) our outlook is cluttered with past pains, regrets, and failures, and 3) the path to what we envision is hampered by the excuses and reasons why we are unable, or have yet to live up what it is we truly desire to create. Which is exactly why the most important step we can make in the aspiration to *let go of our buts* and excuses is to start nurturing the places within that are riddled with feelings of inadequacy and unworthiness.

We must constantly be aware of all there is to love about ourselves, especially when negative self-talk and judgment run rampant in our minds. In order for us to reach the fruition of our greatest desires and aspirations, we have to be willing to show ourselves acts of kindness on a regular basis. We must be gentle and compassionate with the woman we see in the mirror every morning and evening. Remember, how we view ourselves is exactly how we view the world. How we perceive ourselves is how the world will perceive us. How we experience ourselves is how we experience life. It is our responsibility to disallow destructive criticism, judgment, and condemnation to cloud our perception of possibility. It is vitally important that we begin to see and cultivate all that is good and loving about ourselves before we can even begin to require or demand love and respect from others around us. How we love ourselves is how we teach others to love us. To expect anything different is unreasonable. What we believe to be possible in our lives is resultant of how we feel, think, and treat ourselves.

The biggest struggle we must overcome as women is the challenge of loving and accepting ourselves with all of our imperfections. Often, we are the most critical people in our lives. We are quick to discredit everything we have yet to become, and very slow to focus on the things we have done and are doing "right" in our lives. Because of our tendency to concentrate on who we *are not*, and what we have yet to accomplish, we seek validation and approval from others (peers, family members, parents, teachers, etc.) without realizing that they are only going to reflect to us what we already believe to be true and possible for ourselves on the inside.

No amount of talent, skill, positive self-talk, or visioning alone will enable us to illustrate the level of potential we possess when we are lovingly tapped into our truth and our purpose. Nor can we ever be in full alignment with our truth and purpose unless the thoughts, words, beliefs, feelings, perceptions, and yes of course, the actions we choose are also in agreement. Instead, we can muster the courage to love ourselves enough to work at healing past pains derived from mistakes, failures, and regrets. We must be willing to heal the aspects of ourselves that were wounded in previous experiences and have prevented us from being whole and healthy individuals. We must be willing to be more self-aware and honest about why we choose to settle for "less than" rather than moving beyond justifications that impede our path to greatness.

I want to mention something briefly before I move forward. And that is, the issue of mistaking comfort and contentment for fulfillment. I am not referencing the women in the world who are *really* "okay" with where they are in life. I am speaking to women who are ignoring the small voice that says "there is more" to be done. *Ignoring the hushed urge inside you means that you are neglecting to recognize how comfort and contentment serve as the root cause of your inability to overcome excuses. It also blinds you from seeing opportunities to have, be, experience, or bring forth more of who we really are.* What we often miss is that sometimes the "sense of arrival" merely serves as a reflection of our desire to live in the space of self-gratification. What would happen if we were to, instead, use comfort and contentment as motivational mile stones that can ultimately push us beyond limitations?

One of my greatest sources of inspiration at this stage of my life is ultra-marathon runner, David Goggins, known today as one of the toughest men alive. Look at what he has to say about reaching the state of comfort in the quest for achievement:

> *...so, I'm always sharpening my sword and how I sharpen my sword is I have a mentality of 'my refrigerator is never full'. I've never arrived... and every time I get close to the top of the mountain... I fall back down on purpose...I believe that the true growth is at scratch. Starting from scratch is true growth. You have to have friction in your life. There has to be friction in your life for you to be able to move forward.*

I encourage you to keep this in mind if ever you find yourself getting comfortable or feeling as though you have arrived to your destination. Until your last breath, your life is never done. There is always more to do and more to become.

Now, if you will allow, I would like to introduce to you a few perspectives about achievement that may not have been in your immediate awareness. My intention is to help you reach new levels of seeing, thinking, believing, being, and doing so that your cause for greatness becomes greater than your need for comfort. In my research over the years, I have discovered that there are five essential stages to creating the life we desire. Beneath each stage of self-actualization (Level 5 being the lowest and Level 1 the highest) are terms or principles that will be referenced and expounded upon later throughout the series.

Level 5: Fruition and Fulfillment (our lowest form of actualization)

> The more mindful we are of everything we are fortunate enough to have accomplished through the constant effort of loving ourselves and others, the more we are led to discover who we really are at the core of our being. The more we can bring into fruition our greatest desires, the more fulfilling our lives will become. The more fulfilling our lives become, the

more we are compelled to uncover greater aspects of ourselves that will ultimately serve a purpose beyond our own sense of gratification. It all starts with having a clearly defined understanding of the following:

- True Desire
- Success
- Potential
- Purpose
- Health/Healing
- Abundance/Wealth
- Peace
- Wisdom
- Enthusiasm
- Expansion/Evolution
- Compassion/Passion

Level 4: Openness, Gratitude, and Allowance

All of our external experiences, relationships, achievements, and successes come into our lives based on how we allow ourselves to operate in alignment with our highest, most innate aspirations that serve a purpose beyond our own lives. This is achieved through our willingness to express love and gratitude for everything that occurs in our lives - the great outcomes, as well as the outcomes that may not turn out as pleasant as we'd hoped. Full comprehension of what it means to remain open and in the state of gratitude and allowance begins with developing and mastering the following principles:

- Offering /Giving/Sharing
- Creating
- Choosing
- Attracting
- Receiving
- Relieving
- Releasing

Level 3: Release of Negativity

The more we are able to remove or release negativity in our lives, the more space we have for creating radiant health, wealth, abundance, relaxation, peace, joy, and love. This practice will dramatically improve the quality in the most significant aspects of our lives, which include our emotional, mental, physical, spiritual, relational, and financial well-being. The release of negativity begins with incorporating the following practices into our daily lives:

- Connecting feelings to the physical sensations experienced through our body when situations and circumstances arise
- Refraining from using buts, excuses, and justifications for shortcomings and failures
- Refuting the urge to judge the past and dread the future
- Avoid complaining
- Releasing fear and pain from past experiences
- Finding purpose in resistance (there is always a message or lesson to be learned when we pause and take note of what is not occurring or transpiring as we prefer)
- Shifting negative emotions to positive emotions

Level 2: True Perspective Gained

To the degree or level in which we are able to shape our experiences is the way in which we will encounter life's responses. In this context, it is most important to start learning how to have an honest and healthy perspective about ourselves and who we have become as a result of where we've been. Our ability to do this lovingly will then lead us into holding and sharing ourselves lovingly with the world around us. We

do this by becoming more and more mindful of our:
- Feelings/Emotions
- Beliefs
- Perceptions/Outlook (seeking the positive and goodness in all things, people, and circumstances)
- Thoughts
- Degree of Authenticity (complete honesty and truth about who we really are and everything that has occurred or is occurring)

Level 1: Attainment of the *Highest* Aspiration

Our most innate desire, and the power behind what we attract into our lives, is love. Swami Kripalu (a devoted yogi who generated teachings largely around cultivating personal health, well-being, and a virtuous character) said it best: "The highest spiritual aspiration is self-observance with love." Self-observations helps with uncovering patterns, choices and decisions that, even when acted upon unconsciously, somehow govern our lives. Minimizing judgment about our actions helps us to be mindful of how we offer, exist in, and experience our lives. As we strive to continuously lift our minds, hearts, and spirits to the height of unconditional love and gratitude, our lives begin to expand, and our aspirations become more achievable. To do this is to understand the true meaning of love, and the ways through which love, in its purist state, is expressed.

- Love/Gratitude Expression:
    - Practice self-love (being accountable to creating the things in life that bring you happiness, in spite of who or what is occurring around you)
    - Offer the best version of yourself possible (this is love offered to others through and as you)

- Remain open and receptive to love offered by others
- Happiness
- Inspiration
- Kindness/Empathy/Compassion
- Worthiness

Most of us have made the mistake of starting our journey toward fulfillment at Level 5 in hopes of simultaneously achieving Level 1, all the while skipping Levels 4, 3 and 2 entirely. True fulfillment of a life desired takes more than working hard to reach goals and aspirations. Again, we have to ask ourselves if the results of our hard work leave us feeling full, worthy, purposeful, and alive. Or, does it leave us feeling depleted and exhausted? Does the journey to fruition truly satisfy the innate urges to be of service to the world and to create effective change in the lives of others around us? Does it positively impact lives beyond our own? The answers to these questions may be yes; however, it is wise to consider what will come of our lives *after* we have reached our goals and aspirations. This will help us to see what aspects of ourselves need expansion beyond the need for self-gratification. The more this is possible, the more we can stretch our minds to envision all that is possible. As we gain more clarity around the irrefutable influence we have been assigned to contribute to the world through our gifts, talents, and abilities, we become more compelled to overcome the excuses that impede our path to achievement.

Allowing ourselves to really consider our goals from the perspective of serving lives beyond our own is the key to leading a fulfilling life. Even with a goal as small as losing weight (I suppose that is a relative statement, however, I will use the analogy for the sake of contemplation), the most loving thing we can do is to consider what our lives will be like once we have been able to reach our desired weight and size, and how this will positively affect the lives of others in the world around us. Allow me to paint a clearer picture through the following points:

- There is a power in connection (to be discussed in a subsequent chapter) that exists whether we remain conscious of it or not. We are walking epicenters of influence and change. What we do always affects someone else. In this scenario, we are responsible for loving ourselves toward a desired weight, size, or state of health so that others may recognize in us what is possible within themselves.

- Even without being purposeful in our actions, others are always watching. So how we follow through with reaching our desired weight is most certainly inspiring someone else to do the same. How we neglect to follow through with our weight loss goals will spark some sense of discouragement in the lives of those around us.

- We can choose to be more conscious of how we intend to maintain our desired weight once we have reached it. This automatically charges us with the task of staying on the path of health and wellness, rather than saying, "Goal reached. I can go back to my unhealthy lifestyle." Hopefully this is not the case.

- We can also openly share our experiences with others. This is an easy way to hold ourselves in the space of accountability and it also puts us in the position to inspire others, as well as receive the inspiration we need to stay the course. We can blog, write a book, start a fitness group, launch a healthy cooking channel, workout with our children, or create a social media forum for other women who aspire to reach the same achievements.

-

The above statements are some simple ways to maintain accountability as we set out to accomplish goals, while at the same time positively impacting lives beyond our own. With a small shift in perspective, reaching a desired outcome creates a much more expanded experience of inspiration, love, wellness, support, and gratification in your life, and also in the world around us.

Here's something else to consider: *finding the courage to push through barriers, excuses, and limitations is monumental in the quest for experiencing "more" in our lives.* However, our biggest accomplishment is getting to know who we really are, as well as learning how to embrace and love ourselves in spite of flaws and imperfections. Imagine what our lives could become should we choose to love ourselves as we struggle and stumble clumsily along the road to success. The day we can do this is the day we will realize that the need to justify, explain, and make excuses for what we have been unable to do or accomplish up until this point no longer serves us. The focus of loving ourselves and being unapologetic about accepting ourselves entirely automatically propels us into action.

Love invites growth, wisdom, resources, and desired outcomes, while the lack of love (fear) limits, restricts, and blocks the flow of whatever is required in our lives in order to experience fulfillment. It's what triggers the law of attraction (covered in a subsequent chapter called *Love's Law)* which essentially helps us to gain a sense of liberation.

The question is: *how* can we begin the journey of loving ourselves, transcending shame or judgment, and being unapologetic about accepting ourselves entirely? The following is a list of ways you can begin to nurture this process in your own life.

- Stop comparing yourself to others.

- Be willing to open yourself up to doing considerate deeds for others - especially those deeds that speak to the aspects of yourself that is in need of healing and comfort.

- Let go of the past. Forgive yourself for past mistakes and poor choices or decisions. Forgive yourself for having allowed others to mistreat you. Forgive those who chose to act in ways that were not in alignment with your understanding of love.

- Shift your *self*-perception to one of goodness, health, love, and worthiness rather than victimization or defeat.

- Begin <u>each</u> day with an act of love and gratitude for who you are, what you have accomplished, and who you will become.

- Meditate (in whatever form that works best for you, i.e. breathing, walking, reflecting, journaling, sitting still, etc.). The intention is to find ways you can reflect on and release the past, decrease stress levels, and/or enhance your perspective of what is true and what is not true about yourself and the world.

- Be willing to be utterly honest - perceptually, mentally, and emotionally - about what has or has not occurred in your life. Once you can do this, the next step entails being fully accountable for everything that exists in your life, no matter who else was involved. This may take some time. Be patient with yourself. Grant yourself the permission to fully massage the meaning of "being completely responsible for what you have or have not allowed."

- Take ownership of your life. Own your talent. Own your gifts. Own your passion. Own your potential. Own your purpose. Own the lessons you have learned because of your mistakes. Own your place in life, for you are exactly where you need to be to get where you desire to go.

- Start trusting and relying on your intuition. This will help you nurture the process of making healthier choices and decisions.

- Be excited about possibilities and the time you *still* have to create *exactly* what you desire.

- Be pure, clear, concise, and true with your intentions. Monitor the purity behind why you are speaking, thinking, doing, and being about something. Make sure that they are always in alignment with what you desire to achieve or experience in life.

- Remain grateful for everything - the good and even the not so good - in your life.

- Take 15 minutes to a half an hour each day to work on personal and spiritual development. This alone will help you grow and expand exponentially. It is recommended that you do this at the start of each day.

- Be active. Get healthy. Try new things to keep your body moving, your mind alert, and your stress levels down. Exercise is your medication.

- Honor yourself by choosing only to participate in relationships, events, and situations that are respectful and promote wellness.

Love's Law

"For every action, there is an equal and opposite reaction."

- Isaac Newton

*M*y hope is to successfully demonstrate how being aware of our ability, or inability, to offer love, and more importantly, to love ourselves as uncompromisingly as we are, immediately changes our experience of life and how we perceive the world by which we are surrounded. Some of us have reached an inevitable point in our lives where something has to give. Arriving to such an awareness is commendable; however, determining which aspects of our lives need shifting, shaping, or removing may be an extremely difficult task entirely - especially in the moment of overwhelm and discontent. For your own respective journey, I encourage you to begin digesting the meaning behind the following declaration: *Whatever you feel, think, perceive, and believe to be true is, and will always be, reflected in your external life. Whatever you feel, think, perceive, and believe to be true **about yourself** is, and will always be, reflected in your **experience** of life.*

Many of us remain oblivious to how maintaining limited

perspectives of what we believe to be possible are spawned by the unhealthy thoughts and perceptions we hold about who we are. Our reasons for uttering excuses that temporarily justify our shortcomings are rooted in our inclination to sabotage potential outcomes as a way of avoiding failure and rejection. Often times this happens before we even attempt to endeavor a path that leads us from dream to fruition.

This means that before we can begin to understand our reasoning behind self-sabotaging actions and behaviors, or even the *buts,* justifications, and excuses we use to validate deficiency, we must first begin to realize where in our lives we are being unloving. This entails having the courage to stand in our pain and be accountable for what we are tolerating, excusing, allowing, or enabling ourselves to treat our mind, body, and heart unkindly. It also requires being accountable for what we are tolerating or being mindful of when we allow others to treat our minds, bodies and hearts unkindly. We must also begin to identify the parts of ourselves that hinders us from standing fully in our power - to rise above fear and perceived limitations.

Cultivating mindfulness about how unkindly we treat ourselves will help us gain insight on how to move forward in our lives much more lovingly. This is the first step to take in order to lead ourselves into a more fulfilling existence. The insight we need can be garnered when we are willing to reflect on some of the internal inquiries listed below. What I would suggest is that you take a moment to sit alone, in a quiet space with minimal distractions. I would even pull out a pen and a journal to jot down some of the thoughts that arise consequent to contemplation. As you do this, I also encourage you to breathe deeply and allow yourself to *hear* exactly what it is you need in this moment to take the next "right step" toward loving yourself more fully.

- Sit still and reflect on your past. Deliberate over the choices and decisions you've made that have led to this very moment of your life. Also, contemplate some of the current choices and decisions you are in the process of making, and to consider where they can potentially lead you in the future.

- Evaluate aspects of your life that are or are not working. Be honest with yourself. Change transpires the moment you decide to confront the truth head-on.

- Assess which of your relationships no longer support you or your desire to experience more, better, and greater aspects of who you really are.

- Determine where in your life you are choosing, living, and being small, or well beneath your potential.

- Identify whether your job or career path are in alignment with what you truly desire to have, be, or experience in life.

- Contemplate moments in your life where you have treated yourself unlovingly or unkindly, or even where you have allowed others to follow suit and cause you to feel insecure and unworthy of what you truly desire to have, experience, and become.

- Reflect on all the times you have used a "but" to explain why a desired outcome or experience has yet to make its way into your life. Consider whether or not your comfort is greater than your will to love yourself enough to fulfill *your* dreams and aspirations.

Why am I asking you to think about these things?

Well, the more you begin to get a clear understanding of what is or is not serving you, or your life, the more you will be able to reflect on what is compelling you to allow these things to remain, as well as hinder you from creating what you truly desire. The most responsible action in the process of change involves taking ownership of what is playing out in your life. The moment you can do this is the moment you will truly realize the power of choice. As you transition from reflection to revelation, you will be presented with an opportunity to make a different selection or decide to pursue alternative possibilities. Remember, opting to reflect doesn't necessarily give you permission to judge what may very well be unloving or unkind choices, but rather allows you to focus on the possibility for growth and healing.

Changing how you feel about yourself, as well as the circumstances taking place around you, is not always easy if you are accustomed to entertaining negative self-talk and criticism or choosing in ways that are destructive. Here are some points to consider as you begin to make the shift of offering yourself to the world as love:

- Have an honest conversation with yourself about *what love is* to you and how you desire for it to be displayed in your life – from yourself, and then from others. Be specific. It's the only way you'll be able to measure whether your choices and decisions are in alignment with what you deem loving.

- Love yourself *fully*. Start with making the decision to do so always and in *all ways* - compassionately and unapologetically.

- Learn exactly what it is you have to contribute to this world. Envision how you will go about making a unique contribution to the world during your lifetime. Once you have done so, make every effort to ensure that your thoughts, choices, beliefs, and actions remain in alignment with a fervent intention to carry out the vision.

- Know that what you give to the world will come back to you equally.

- Choose to have an optimistic perception or outlook of what you have or have not attracted into your life.

- Remember: *Nothing* exists in your life if it was not first invited - consciously or otherwise.

- Trust without any doubt that everything you encounter is meant to teach you a lesson through which the wisdom you obtain can be applied towards greater things that will be able to create later in life. To understand this is to recognize what and why you are attracting certain people, relationships, circumstances, and situations. Remember, whatever you encounter is life's way of responding to something you are consciously or unconsciously requesting, thinking, or believing.

- Evaluate the not so good perspectives you maintain about who you are, as well as, what has become of your life, so the awareness about the aspects of yourself that require healing or more love begins to expand.

- Positively align your thoughts and perceptions about what you believe to be possible through you.

- Happiness and fulfillment grow more abundant the moment you decide to think, speak, believe, and feel in ways that are good and loving.

- The need for excuses to validate rejection and failure ceases to exist when you experience all things in life as love - this includes you.

One of the most significant steps to overcoming challenges and transcending perceived limitations involves learning how to love yourself completely. This entails being accountable for *everything* that occurs in your life, no matter who else may be involved. Loving yourself also entails refuting urges to criticize or judge previous choices, actions, decisions, and behaviors that resulted in undesired situations. To love yourself is to know that you are not your circumstances, but rather a culmination of experiences, which include your thoughts, feelings, and beliefs. To love yourself fully is to recognize that you have made poor choices and decisions, and then make better or wiser choices founded in the lessons and knowledge obtained from painful or contrasting experiences.

Take a few moments to continue reflecting. Again, treat yourself lovingly and avoid drowning in self-criticism. As you do this, keep in mind the following: *Love is the connecting force of positive energy flowing in and through everything existing in the Universe. Not only are you no exception to this principle, you are also worthy of its benefits.*

♥♥♥♥♥

To continue the topic of what we may have allowed or not allowed to come forth in our lives, let's discuss the true context of "but." As we will cover in later chapters, the premise of *buts* and excuses signifies our unwillingness to love ourselves fully or deem ourselves worthy of taking action toward the actualized side of our desires.

How unloving!

If there is nothing else to learn from this series, the one thing we will walk away with is the truth declaring that we deserve to *live* the best, *create* the best, and *have* the best of whatever we desire in life. In the event we ever find ourselves feeling otherwise, it simply means that we have some very significant choices and decisions to make. To feel undeserving of all that is good generally means that we are off course with achieving, attaining, and becoming whatever we have envisioned in our mind, and feel in our soul.

The true essence of love, in this context, stretches well beyond our emotional adoration for a person or being. Each and every one of us has been gifted with the innate yearning for love, a genuine connection with others, and an assignment through which we are designated to carry out our contribution of love. However, the truest sentiment of love doesn't just stop at the affectionate exchange between two people (or more). It extends to situations, circumstances, experiences, hopes, dreams, and desires. Everything we experience in life is resultant of the degree of love we give out or offer. The good we experience in our lives is contingent upon our ability to give love - to ourselves, to life, to the world, and to the Universe.

Though love is not always seen, heard, or felt, it is always operating with or without our awareness. The energy of love is always present and available to exchange, which means that whatever we give out in life is exactly what we will receive back at equal value. I think we can all agree on what it means or feels like to *consciously* offer gestures of love; however, there is no way for us to define the degree of love extended toward us, even if it is done so in ways that we do not prefer. Pain and mistreatment doled out by another does not always mean a person does not love us. It is, however, *our* responsibility to define and communicate what we will or will not allow through our own understanding of love. We are also responsible for living our lives - which includes being mindful of how we treat ourselves - in accordance with what we communicate and define to others. I bring this up simply because we as women have a tendency to focus on the unloving treatment of others, and how it negatively impacts our lives.

This is why it is often times easy for us to get derailed and distracted from carrying out our potential and purpose. Once we have healed, we often learn that attempting to will a person into loving us the way we desire is futile. We have no control over what others may or may not do in the name of love. All we can do is make certain that through our choice to offer (and receive) love, we are always creating a sense of fulfillment, happiness, joy, peace, compassion, freedom, and wellbeing for ourselves and others.

On the other hand, we must also realize that love, or lack thereof, is sometimes extended unconsciously. Often, this tends to be resultant of emotions or feelings that are not out rightly perceived, expressed, or experienced by way of our gestures or conversations, but rather through our thoughts, feelings, and beliefs (which are supported by your feelings) that promote negative and limited perspectives of who we are. Therefore, it is wise to make sure that everything we think, believe, speak, or act upon falls in alignment with our highest understanding of love. Regardless of whether or not we are offering and perceiving love consciously, life will always return to us exactly what and how we are presenting to the world from within. Thus, negative experiences can always serve as indicators that reflect how discontented, or detached, we are feeling about ourselves in a instance.

With such a wonderfully powerful awareness, your effort to maintain responsibility for what does or does not occur through and for you is hopefully more evident. Being consciously accountable for the events that transpire in your life is to understand that life is never happening to you, but rather responding to your thoughts and feelings. It also is embracing the notion that how things play out before you are always directly related to the beliefs and perspectives you are holding about whatever is occurring. I guarantee you this: should you choose to perceive an event or circumstances through the perspective of love and positivity, it will play out much differently than if you had opted to perceive it from a perspective of fear and negativity.

The highest, most innate feeling or emotion in life is love. There is nothing higher. When it comes to living a life of authenticity and achievement, and with greater awareness and accountability, there is truly no other emotion. There is either love or there isn't. Even when referencing negative emotions such as fear, anger, and jealousy, what we are really creating or bringing into our reality is a decrease in, or absence of, love. Until we can love ourselves fully, as well as offer ourselves to the world *authentically as love*, we will never have the life we truly desire. The need to protect or deny aspects of who we really are is far from loving. Remember, our lives, which of course encompass our purpose for being, exist with an objective that is far beyond our own gratification and comfort. Being true to our desires entails letting go of the need to protect ourselves from rejection, failure, and pain. It also entails shedding, or at least confronting, all of the fears (lack of love) that prevent us from devising and attracting everything we need to be successful or reach fulfillment.

Rhonda Bynre, the phenomenal creator of *The Secret* and insightful author of *The Power,* teaches this concept best. She says, "The life of your dreams has always been closer to you than you realize, because the power to have everything good in your life is inside you...if you can feel it, you can receive it."

Truly understanding the concept of love, and the ability to attract our desired lives through love, starts first with learning how to love ourselves. It also begins with believing that a life devoid of regrets, excuses and justifications is possible for you because of loving yourself and offering yourself to the world as love. I will expound more on how to love yourself fully in later volumes. For now, I will share insight on how to determine whether or not you are offering yourself as love, or even allowing yourself to receive the love you need to have a fulfilling life. I'd like to do this by taking a moment to deliberate over the concept of *feelings*.

Essentially, our feelings and emotions help with detecting whether or not we are making a choice that is loving or one that is based on fear. In order to measure our feelings, we must first be able to recognize that there are more emotions or feelings to experience beyond anger, sadness, and happiness. Simply put, we can start by determining what side of, and to what degree of, positivity or negativity we feel when situations and circumstances arise. Good, or positive, feelings are those that are founded in love and arouse a sense of happiness, joy, peace, gratitude, gratification, fulfillment, freedom, compassion, hope, and passion. Not so good, or negative feelings, include those that promote sentiments of anger, worry, frustration, hate, dread, fear, despair, guilt, distress, and shame. Feel free to research emotions in order to discover the whole spectrum of feelings we can potentially experience consequent to the events that transpire throughout our lives - past, current, and future.

Any outcome can *unfold* in our lives in accordance with how we are *feeling* in any given moment. Thus, an outcome as big as an aspiration is often altered or come to fruition based on how we are thinking, feeling, and believing about it. This means that the life we are living today can turn into the life we desire by simply changing how we feel about where we are, what we have, or what we will have but has yet to transpire. The moment we change our focus from seeing, feeling, thinking, and believing negatively about what is happening, the fate of our lives will change. As soon as we decide to change our feelings from not so good to good, the past we regret, the current situation we despise, and the future we dread all cease to exist. The only thing that will remain is the love through which we have the capacity to create exactly what we desire -through which the perpetual sense of gratitude and enthusiasm enhances our experience of life altogether. With that, all we have to do is be present in the moment and make the choice to be and do something better and greater than we already are. Everything else we need will line up for us in accordance to our outlook.

The blessings, resources, and relationships that are required to support the fruition of an intended outcome are either blocked or drawn to us based on how we perceive or experience them. They are also blocked or allowed into our lives at the level in which we feel deserving or worthy. Perceiving a current circumstance or future aspiration through the lens of love and enthusiasm is to say, "Hey!!! Come on in! I can't wait to see what we can create together!" Perceiving a current circumstance or future aspiration through the lens of dread and despair is like saying, "Hey! You know, I see you, and even though I want you in my life, it is best you stay where you are for now." See the difference in approach? We have the power to attract into our lives the people, events, and circumstances required to bring an aspiration into fruition by being mindful of how we are feeling, and then making sure our actions and beliefs are in alignment. And this occurs to the degree in which we can capture an event through the lens of fear or love. The wider our love lens, the more invigorating our experiences will be. The wider our fear lens, the more distressed our experiences will be.

I am attempting to point out the correlation between how you may be feeling about yourself and a relationship, situation, or circumstance, and the tendency to use *buts* when speaking of your aspirations and desires. Think about it, *buts* do not promote good or positive feelings. Excuses and justifications only set you up to feel more of the negativity caused by your experience of failure or rejection. In all of my years, I have never heard anyone excitedly share reasons why a desired experience has yet to come to fruition. *Buts* negate your worthiness for whatever it is you desire to have, be, or experience. Using excuses only validates a willingness to forfeit a true desire to feelings of unworthiness. This alone is extremely unloving. The expression of justifications for shortcomings and failures usually comes with feelings of shame, guilt, regret, and fear (again, the opposite of love). However, one thing is for certain: *the circumstances of your life will remain the same if you continue to justify them.* At some point, you will grow to realize that the conditions in your life that hinder you from progress and fulfillment will never get better until you *feel* better about them. The sooner you can *feel* better, the sooner you can get on with choosing more loving tasks that will get you re-aligned with what you truly desire.

Changing our feelings can happen instantly, or it can take some practice. However, doing the best we can to focus on the positive aspects of our lives rather than on what is seemingly not working is a great start. In short, to love ourselves is to know that we can create our lives *exactly* as we envision it. Instead of trying to change our lives in one sweeping shift, igniting a sense of overwhelm and discouragement, we can practice managing our feelings about people, environments, circumstances, conditions, and situations. For those feelings we can pinpoint as good or positive, we can strive to cultivate more of them by way of offering ourselves to the world as love. For those feelings that are not so good, we can practice making new choices and new decisions that enable us to change a circumstance to one that is better or greater.

The Four A's

"Fear is a natural reaction to moving closer to the truth."

- Pema Chodron

    *T*here is an extremely poignant truth to consider as we continue our discussion on loving ourselves into full potential: *some of the most difficult challenges we have in life are the ones we create on our own.* Now mind you, half of the time we don't recognize that we are on the path of suffering and potential destruction, until we are on the despised side of our desires. Aside from that, we aren't always aware that we are, in fact, creating the problems that transpire in our lives by way of the limited perspectives and attitudes we hold about whatever is or is not occurring in our lives. And then, there are also those times where we *are* completely aware of the potential for a choice or decision made to result in problems that interfere with long-standing goals. Though associating choices, decisions, and actions to self-defeating consequences can sometimes lessen the number of challenges we endure, it doesn't always mean we will have the ability to disengage from specific behaviors that limit potential. We often manage to interfere with our progress towards our dreams and aspirations through maintaining some of the following beliefs and behaviors:

Negative Beliefs

1. This won't work.
2. It's not possible.
3. I can't do this.
4. I'm too busy right now.
5. I'm just not ready yet.
6. I'm not good enough.
7. I don't have what I need.
8. I need more money, time, and knowledge.
9. I must to do "this" before I can do "that."

Limiting Behaviors

1. Committing to the fear of failure instead of eagerly approaching a potential lesson or fruitful experience.
2. Refusing to take risks and make mistakes.
3. Dismissing constructive criticism from others who may be more knowledgeable or experienced.
4. Neglecting to hold the vision of a and plan out my life accordingly.
5. Remaining inflexible when considering solutions to challenges and problems.
6. Failing consider consequences and repercussions of choices and decisions.
7. Constantly worrying without taking the time to consider alternative options that alleviate stress and anxiety.
8. Placing blame on and complain about people, situations, and

circumstances without ever looking within for opportunities to be accountable.
9. Holding unrealistic expectations.
10. Criticizing, and then judging, all mistakes and failures while making comparisons to the lives of others.
11. Refusing to adapt when faced with opposition.
12. Procrastinating and making excuses, justifications, and rationalizations for why something is or is not transpiring.
13. Maintaining negative perspectives about the things that do or do not occur.
14. Focusing only on the things that are "going wrong" verses everything that *is* working in my life.

    I think each and every one of us can attest to the fact that it is easy to get caught up in encouraging ourselves to overcome fears, or pursuing a passion in spite of unpleasant circumstances, as long as things are working out according to what we envision. Yet, what happens when if we fail? What happens when things fall apart and don't come to fruition as we'd hoped? Most of us are guilty of engaging with some of the limiting behaviors and negative beliefs that are listed above. Remembering to love ourselves beyond what we perceive, and experience, negatively doesn't come easy. Nevertheless, one thing is for certain: maintaining self-defeating perspectives or mindsets is extremely unloving and perpetuates misalignment in our lives. As much as we think loving ourselves comes through our attempt to be perfect and free of failure, self-sabotage is congruent with the belief that we are deficient or undeserving in some way. There is nothing wrong with wanting to "get it right" or to succeed at something on the first, second, or third attempt. The damage, however, is incurred when we allow ourselves to be overwhelmed with discouragement and lose our focus, when we neglect to remember who we really are, or when we recommit to the habit of judging and criticizing ourselves harshly when we fall short.

More on the self-sabotaging belief systems and how to overcome them will be covered later on in the series. Since the objectives highlighted throughout this volume are centered on remembering and re-aligning with who we really are, remaining mindful of choices, decisions, beliefs, perspectives, conversations, or actions, and more importantly, loving ourselves truly, is paramount to our desire for fulfillment. With that said, we should make extra effort to grow more mindful of the ways we can enable ourselves to get off the cyclical path of destruction. True, this process begins with learning how to love ourselves completely, but it doesn't stop there. It also entails finding the courage to stop the suffering caused by our resistant patterns in order to allow joy, love, well-being, and success to flow in and through our lives. The keyword in the previous statement is *allow,* which is the opposite of resistance or rejection. Because we are not always aware of what thoughts and beliefs we hold about ourselves or a particular experience, we sometimes remain blinded by our tendency to create shields and roadblocks. For some of us who are overachievers, the inclination here would be to defensively inquire, "How is this possible when I do everything in my power to achieve my goals or go after whatever I want in life?" My question to you then would be: if this is truly the case, why is it that you have yet to start *fully* living and experiencing the life you envision?

There are some pretty good answers to this question. Yet, we must first decide, and then commit to, exercising our freedom to choose something different than what we are already doing, seeing, perceiving, believing, and knowing. This is possible once we have a deeper understanding of the following principles and how they play a significant part in the way our lives unfold.

Acceptance
"Accept what is, let go of what was, and have faith in what will be."

~Sonia Ricotti

Do not be mistaken into thinking that acceptance means submitting to or approving circumstances that you do not prefer or desire. The term here refers to the "*is-ness*" of things as they are, without judgment, shame, or guilt. The opposing choice to acceptance is resistance, which causes suffering and misery. Refusing to entirely accept circumstances as they are, or admit to and affirm who you have become, prohibits the process of learning whatever is required for you to move forward. The result of your refusal to accept is simple: the experience of creating and allowing more of what you are reluctant to accept. That is, until you are willing to change your mind. Acceptance (non-resistance) moves you towards experiencing things as they are meant to be experienced, feeling completely happy with yourself from the inside out, and then embracing changes that may need to occur for you to move from one state of being into the next. Acceptance empowers you to expand your understanding of the world, your life, and your circumstances. It enables you to focus on the positive side of things, as well as the opportunities and resources designed to support your aspirations that will begin to appear as your perspective of life begins to expand.

Here are some points to help maintain the ability to accept things in your life *as they are* so that you may move forward in or from situations and relationships that appear to be hindering your growth and progress:

- You are right where you are supposed to be, regardless of how undesirable the circumstances appear.
- Every event, incident, or situation in your life is designed to teach you whatever is required for transition and transcendence.
- Everything and everyone in your life exists with reason and purpose.
- Nothing in your life has transpired, is transpiring, or will transpire without you first inviting it in or allowing it to subsist.
- Nothing stays the same. Everything changes. Every experience you have is bound to evolve or dissolve according to your thoughts, perceptions, beliefs, and decisions.

Alignment
"Don't look for the solution. Look for alignment. It will bring the solution."

- Abraham Hicks

In this context, alignment means that all of your beliefs, perspectives, thoughts, emotions, and actions are all lined up in accordance with whatever it is you desire in a specific moment, or in your overall life. When this happens, often times there is a sense of feeling good, relaxed, happy, peaceful, and enthusiastic about what is "coming." The strong sense of "need" dissipates as a result of you remaining open to having your desires come to life in ways you may or may not have fathomed. Alignment eliminates the urge to know "how" things will transpire. Practicing being in alignment is not always easy; however, it does help with gaining momentum towards fruition and manifestation of things desired.

Here are some ways to know when you are in alignment with your true self, which embodies your deepest desires and aspirations:

- Regardless of what is or is not occurring, you are always excited and never doubtful.
- You remain relaxed, instead of anxious or strained, when things are not be unfolding as you prefer.
- You are faithfully focused, undoubtedly knowing that things will work out or come to fruition as intended.
- You maintain an enthusiastic attitude rather than a negative or discouraging outlook in the face of challenges.
- You are patient, fully believing that what you desire will come into your life at the right time.
- Through the ability to accept things as they are, feelings of disappointment and rejection fall away to your commitment to cultivate peace, wisdom, and compassion.
- You use negative emotions as indicators to help you know when you are out of alignment with what you desire and prefer, and immediately make another choice or decision to point you in the right direction.

Attraction

"You attract to you everything you require according to the nature of your thought life. Your environment, relationships, and financial conditions are

the perfect reflections of your habitual thinking."

- Joseph Murphy

To maintain contextual alignment with the previous principle, we will sum up this term to mean that "like attracts like." Every experience playing out in your life has been something you either attracted or invited through your thoughts and beliefs - however negative, positive, love-based, or fear-based they may be. This mindset is based on the notion that you and your thoughts are made up of energy. Everything existing within this wide Universe is also made up of energy. Thus, your environments, relationships, and financial conditions are playing out in your life as a result of your thought-energy attracting the like-energy of things, people, and circumstances that will essentially support the manifestation of whatever you are thinking. Simply put, you attract whatever it is you think about. Incorporating this perspective and awareness into your life naturally makes you accountable for everything that occurs within it.

Allowance

"Allowance entails doing whatever you can to let life, people, and situations be as they are in spite of challenge and opposition. In turn, you become capable of adjusting your dominant thoughts and feelings to align with whatever is required to bring a desired result or outcome into fruition."

- Naje Badu

Learning to allow things, people, and circumstances to be as they are without judgment or criticism is not always easy; however, your ability to master this practice results in not having to force desired experiences into your life. Remember, this also includes formidable situations that arise consequent to choices and decisions you have made or did not make. Practicing the art of allowance alleviates the *need* to resist discomfort. It urges you to move beyond fears and comfort zones. Guilt, shame, and regret cease to exist when you are able to allow experiences to be exactly as they are, and then release them for the sake of retaining and applying the lesson acquired. Judgment and negative self-talk are also released the moment you *give yourself permission* to be more than your circumstances.

Here are just a few positive statements that support the practice of allowance in your daily life:

- I allow myself to request and ask for whatever it is I desire.
- I allow myself to voice my feelings about whatever I am experiencing as long as they are healthy and helpful, rather than harmful, to others.
- I allow myself to venture through my own process of healing from rejection, failure, and mistakes, and not what someone else has deemed healthy.
- I allow experiences to be exactly as they are without creating suffering in my life or the lives of others by way of negative thoughts, self-criticism, blame, or guilt.
- I allow others to have their opinions without judgment.
- I release whatever I am unable to change or control.
- I release the *need* to control what does not affect me or my life by allowing myself to focus on positive change, progress, and evolution.
- My greatest contribution to the things, people, and situations I am unable to change is to focus on love and pray for the highest good for everyone involved.

Feel free to use your journal to jot down some statements of your own that will empower you to move through specific trials or challenges by practicing allowance.

To sum it all up, *accepting* and embracing the perfection and beauty (even if you cannot see it with the physical eye) of where you stand today leads to healing. Acceptance enables you to see life, and everything occurring within, as an orchestration of all that is designed to guide you toward higher and greater circumstances, which will ultimately teach you the lessons required for growth and progress. *Allowance* is a true act of courage and a testament of trust and belief that something is always occurring and evolving for your good. *Alignment* relieves you from the needing preferred conditions to exist prior to reaching states of joy, happiness, excitement, and enthusiasm. Being mentally (thoughts), physically (actions and behaviors), emotionally, and spiritually aligned with what you truly desire builds momentum towards fulfillment, creation, and expression. It helps with understanding, and then implementing, the practice of feeling good despite circumstances in order to create, as well as attract preferred conditions into your life.

♥♥♥♥♥

Spiritual advisors and vision coaches will be the first to proclaim that "alignment trumps everything." The lining-up of our thoughts, actions, beliefs, and perceptions in accordance to desired outcomes and aspirations eclipses even those things in our lives that we experience as loathsome or not working out as we previously envisioned.

Here is a perfect opportunity to discuss briefly the concept of accepting *is-ness*, which I believe is the second most compelling reason (the first being an inability to love ourselves fully and unapologetically) why we miss the mark when it comes to dreams and aspirations. *Is-ness,* in this context, can be paradoxically defined in two ways: 1) the state of things as they are elementally and factually, without judgments, labels, stories, or conclusions, and 2) the level of awareness that says everything that exists, or comes into our physical experience, is already existing in a non-physical realm.

Read this next paragraph slowly. I would also urge you to read it two or three times and let it sink in before moving on.

> *Is-ness is the continuation of our being-ness that extends beyond the visible and into the invisible aspects of life. Creation is not only occurring in the*

> *physical realm. Who we are meant to become is not only unfolding in the physical realm. The fact that we are able to live out thoughts, ideas, and dreams experientially does not negate the potential for things desired to be created prior to it being allowed into our minds, let alone our lives. Our being-ness often surpasses our mental comprehension of what it means to create whatever we desire. The objective is to begin incorporating this awareness into our daily lives so that we may be truly empowered to love ourselves into full potential and possibility, without limitation or hindrance.*

That is a lot to take in and grasp at one time; however, I encourage you to sit with it. Come back to it from time to time until it resonates. In our spiritual practices, this concept is equivalent to "having faith beyond understanding." Subscribing to this perspective itself is enough to align ourselves with the notion that what we desire and require already exists. Once we can fully comprehend the meaning and value of the insight shared above, we can then begin to understand why our dreams prove to be the greatest examples of *"is-ness"* in our lives. If we were to think back for a second and reflect on all of the aspirations and desires we ever held, we would probably realize that most of them eventually came to fruition as time progressed. This means that everything we ever envisioned or desired that came to fruition was at one point merely a preconceived vision of what "could be." If we were to go further and ponder over all the desires, or aspirations, we have been able to achieve, we will discover that the obstacles between us and a dream fulfilled was overcome by putting the following practices into place:

- **Maintaining Extreme Focus** - *adjusting outlooks and perceptions and zeroing in on what "could be."*

- **Accepting What Is** - *acknowledging the possibility that whatever was being envisioned actually existed and the only thing that could potentially impede fruition was you.*

- **Maintaining Alignment** - *thinking, feeling, and believing in accordance to the desired outcome.*

- **Remaining Open to Attract Whatever is Required** - *remaining open to receive everything required to support your quest for fulfillment.*

- **Mastering the Art of Allowance** - *releasing negativity and limited perspectives to create space for a possibility and potentiality.*

As we continue to practice a*cceptance, alignment, attraction, and allowance,* the need to base our beliefs in the fruition of something envisioned only on physical evidence falls away. Instead, we begin choosing to move through challenging encounters holding anticipation, *a deep sense of knowing,* for something bigger, brighter, or more in alignment with what we prefer. When tapped into this type of mindset, we are no longer susceptible to the disappointment of unmet expectations and outcomes. We allow ourselves to see beyond face value. We relinquish all attachments to how outcomes *should* arise. We become empowered through the flow of our creativity. We develop a confident belief in the trustworthiness of ourselves, of each other, and of the Universe. We establish trust in our ability to make healthy choices and decisions. Our feelings begin to serve as instruments for momentum and perpetuation of the belief that everything good *is,* and *subsists,* to support our process of becoming exactly what we envision. Ultimately, we become more inclined to love ourselves enough to let go of the *buts* that hinder our progress and growth.

A moment ago, I mentioned the practice of *exercising the*

freedom to choose something different; something other than what we are already doing, seeing, perceiving, believing, and knowing. This is best accomplished when we are able to let go of what we *think* we know, tap into the multitude of possibilities that exist beyond our comprehension, and allow the things to cease and emerge naturally, by accepting them as they *are* - not as they were or could be. Holding belief in the possibility of something that has yet to enter our physical experience is a way of acknowledging its *"is-ness."* It is through the act of maintaining such a belief that we can move a concept, idea, or thought from imagination to reality.

Let's face it, most of us tend to develop perceptions, beliefs, and thoughts about what is possible based on what we are able to experience and express through sight, sound, and touch. We use our senses, as well as our memories, as proof of what can or cannot be created, altered, or enhanced. We use the perceptions of our current conditions and circumstances to dictate our ability, or inability, to achieve our aspirations. We have grown accustomed to relying on what we are able to perceive today to determine what is or is not possible in the future. For any of us to rise above physical and mental limitations, it would behoove us to begin heavily considering the things that exist beyond sight, sound, or touch.

What exactly do I mean?

Learning to trust in an already existing *is-ness*, despite what we are experiencing in the current moment, helps with emotionally aligning with preferred and desired outcomes by way of maintaining a greater sense of wellbeing. Also, by linking our feelings to desired outcomes in order to gage how far in or out of alignment we are with achievement. Though this can be a very challenging task, it is one that can be easily surmounted when things seem to be going well and happiness percolates from the core of our being. However, the ease of accomplish the task ceases when things don't go well, or when a relationship or situation turns out to be something other than what we preferred or hoped. Nine times out of ten, when the things we envision do not turn out as planned, we lack the energy, the outlook, or even the wherewithal to see beyond what is occurring. It is during these times that it becomes very easy for us to lose focus on the possibility that something other than what we are encountering in the moment exists. It is during those times where believing in something that doesn't appear to be real, true, or possible, becomes extremely enervating and exhausting. If we were wiser, we would pause for a moment and get a greater glimpse of what the resistance is *really* presenting: an opportunity to choose a different path, or, at the very least, focus our energy on making a decision that will stretch us beyond our comfort zones. This is how we grow.

Irrespective to your degree of awareness, here is how life really works: *as soon as a thought is formed in your mind, an emotion is linked to it. Depending on the level of positivity (or negativity) of your thought-feeling connection, you become inclined to move into (taking action) or away from (resisting) the urge to create whatever ideas or visions that may evolve from that initial thought.* Much like belief and faith, the process of envisioning is extremely vital to the actual creation of *is-ness*. Prior to the moment your mind processes a thought, the vision or the desired outcome is already being created. It is your job to remain in the state of a*cceptance, alignment, attraction, and allowance* so that whatever ideas you imagine can come through you. You are an instrument designed and empowered to create exactly what you think. So, continuously practice being aware of your thoughts and beliefs.

By now, you hopefully understand the magnitude behind allowing your thoughts and emotions to move you from an idea to possibility to fruition. Maintaining excitement and anticipation perpetuates the creation of that which has been imagined. This means, if you can conceive it you can achieve it. It's your responsibility to *align, allow, accept, and attract* whatever is required to bring everything you conceive into physical existence. Each time you have a thought that is in alignment with what you desire or prefer, you position yourself to allow, invite, or receive whatever is required to help you create what you envisioned. However, the moment you place a "but" after your thought - spoken or unspoken - the evidence of your alignment comes forth. All momentum of fruition comes to a halt and is prohibited from coming forth into your life until you are able to shift your thoughts, as well as the intensity of your emotions, from doubtfulness to possibility.

If you are not conscious about what you entertain in your mind, pure thoughts can be stunted the moment they are contested by negative beliefs that contradict potentiality and possibility. The evidence of this is littered throughout your life by way of the numerous wants, dreams, goals, and aspirations that have yet to reach full manifestation. Most of your ambitions were possibly annihilated immediately after conception because of simply entertaining *buts*, excuses, rationalizations, and justifications about why whatever you conceived is not doable or possible. Imagine, if you will, what would happen if you refrained from diverting your focus from the impossible to allowing an idea to move naturally through its process of conception to fruition without hindrance. What would happen if you allowed a thought to move toward emotional connection, to strengthened belief, to attraction of resources, to action, and eventually to completion without contradiction?

The objective in your life from this point forward shall be to cultivate love and create enough momentum toward your preferred states of living, being, having, and experiencing. So much so that they have no choice but to come into fruition. Maintaining and increasing your momentum towards manifestation is accomplished by:

- Focusing on, perceiving, and creating positive

experiences
- Cultivating positive thoughts
- Undoubtedly believing in the possibility of all things, concepts, and ideas
- Acting, choosing, and deciding in accordance with true desires, goals, and aspirations
- Developing and maintaining high levels of value and self-worth

Neglecting to practice the aforementioned will cause us to block the blessings and resources that already exist and patiently await our alignment and reception. We inadvertently fall victim to our own negativity and position ourselves to sit in constant wait for something good to happen in our lives in order to overcome stagnation and complacency; or, in order to move through ill-favored situations and circumstances. From this day forward, we must opt out of relying on changes in external conditions to alter how we perceive, believe, think, and act in the face of trials. It is impossible to seek external evidence of happiness and maintain alignment with who we really are at the same time. As we make the decision to maintain positive outlooks and increased levels of ambition, we will begin to notice how the conditions that surround us automatically change.

The practice of feeling good about ourselves and the experiences we have essentially open us up to receive all that is required to maintain a fulfilling life. No longer will we need to prove our happiness through the things we acquire or the relationships we maintain. No longer will we require others to put constant effort into making us feel good about ourselves just to prove their love. We will, instead, recognize the responsibility we have to increase our own levels of value and self-worth. Through this effort, we will be able to shift our attention towards developing and allowing all that is good about ourselves, to emerge in our life experience. Our focus then becomes aligned with getting in touch with our true feelings and emotions. Thus, we begin to expand our belief in a realm of *"is-ness"* that exists beyond sight and sound. In addition to growing the power and scope of our beliefs, we also become aligned with believing in our true potential to create, realize, and bring forth every idea imagined. Consequently, our ability to undoubtedly know, be, experience, or become exactly who we are meant is amplified.

Growing in Grace

"There is no real doing in the world without being first. Being your presence, as well as your connection to yourself and to that which is greater than you, is far more greater than what you do. It is what fuels all that you have been called here to do."

- Oprah Winfrey

I experienced sentiments of remiss each time I considered omitting what I have included in this chapter during the editing phase. I weighed inclusion heavily against waiting to broach the subject of growth and grace in a subsequent volume before finally coming up with the compromise of introducing the following ideas and principles, and then expounding upon them in later volumes. I arrived at this decision after concluding that the information shared can potentially change our perspective of how we see ourselves, our relationships, and the world at large. I have learned through experience that a shift in self-perception ultimately alters our perspective of what is or is not occurring for us.

Changing how we see ourselves not only takes courage and raw honesty, it also helps with discovering hidden strengths, or improving weaknesses, some of which we may not even be aware. I'd like us to keep in mind that every perception we hold of where we are (physically, spiritually, mentally, and emotionally), who we encounter, what we experience, and what we are capable of achieving is influenced by past experiences, beliefs, and expectations. By altering core beliefs, specifically those pertaining to our potential and ability to love ourselves fully, we can change the way we perceive, and then experience, the world around us.

Rising above the mindset of lack or mediocrity (a result of our inclination to lean more on reasons, excuses, and justifications for shortcomings rather than taking action that help us to transcend our limitations) entails more than loving ourselves or holding on to our dreams and aspirations. It takes the ability to completely embrace the notion of owning our own experiences and then relying on the power of love, wisdom, faith, alignment, and connection to move us from one level of fulfillment to the next. We must begin to recognize the freedom that is possible to attain through the practice of choosing and deciding in accordance with what we desire, as well as the discipline of staying focused on goodness and positivity. It involves truly learning and then owning our true potential, even as it begins to look different from the potential of those who surround us. Even then, we must continue to own our true potential as it begins to appear bigger and brighter than what other may believe to be true about us. This is crucial, especially when our potential begins to outgrow all that we have ever conceived of ourselves. In all actuality, we must be willing to march gracefully and purposefully to the beat of our own drums, even when the path gets narrow and our friends become few.

By now, you may be a little more aware of the call to rise to fulfill the purpose residing in your heart; to make bigger contributions through your life. You may not know exactly what it is, but perhaps you have grown certain that something bigger and better for you exists. Otherwise you would not have attracted or created the opportunity to read or listen to this book. Nestled deep within you is the drive that compels you to move beyond negativity and disbelief. There's that "something inside of you" that is pushing you to discover the exact opposite, or an enhanced version, of what you may or may not be experiencing in this moment. I would even preclude that you are at the point where the desire burning deep within is about to erupt and ultimately change the trajectory of your life. Now ask yourself: what could possibly happen if you were to throw caution to the wind and become more self-expressed in what you know to be possible and true about who you really are? What if you hopped off the hamster wheel of complacency and begin following a path that has been paved specifically for you?

When heeded, the whispered wisdom of our beautiful mothers, grandmothers, and ancestors lovingly reminds us that our potential and will to create lives that are above and beyond average is innate within. Because of this, we must do everything in our power to rise above mediocrity for the sake of carving a solid path for our little sisters who are graciously following in our footsteps, eagerly waiting for their chance to carry on the torch of creativity, passion, and purpose. To do this, we must learn how to execute the following:

- Design and define the direction to be followed in order to become who we really are.
- Take all the time we need to reflect and examine our failures in a positive light.
- Search for the lessons learned but ignored, and then re-evaluate what is or is not working in our lives, so that we may make the necessary adjustments along the way.
- Be willing to unlearn mindsets, behaviors, attitudes, and outlooks that were developed during our childhoods, yet no longer serve a purpose.
- Challenge ourselves to replace limited perspectives with those that prove to be positive, profitable, and progressive.
- Become lifelong students and develop an acute thirst for knowledge so that we avoid remaining stuck in the past and unable to contribute value to the lives of others around us.
- Be cognizant of being "big fish in small ponds," and thus empower ourselves to be *that* "fish who lovingly dares to swim out of its comfort zone" for the sake of being more than average.

Based on the hours and hours I have invested studying and absorbing principles and philosophies centered on human behavior, psychology, spirituality, metaphysics, leadership, personal development, and all the training involved with becoming a professional life coach, I have come to learn some ideologies that I believe to be requisites to every woman's burning desire to grow and love themselves gracefully. I have taken the pleasure of sharing them below.

Self-awareness is an essential component to success and fulfillment. It is also one of the most pivotal elements on which to focus as it relates to discerning the ways in which we are, or are not thinking, behaving, deciding, and choosing. Self-awareness helps us identify the areas in our lives where self-love is cultivated within or offered externally. A heightened sense of self-awareness leads to understanding exactly why something is or is not coming into our lives as desired. It is impossible to succeed in anything meaningful or bring an extraordinary vision into fruition without first knowing why we are here and what we have been called to do with our lives, and second, understanding what aspects of ourselves are in or out of alignment with any vision, dream, or aspiration we hold. Sitting still, listening to, adapting, preparing, and then answering life's calling is the most effective way to minimize distraction and discouragement. It is to the degree of our awareness of how we are to contribute to the world that we will experience joy, peace, happiness, abundance, and freedom. Also, it is through our willingness to expand in self-awareness that our perception of how the world occurs will begin to shift from negative to positive.

We must be authentic in our choice to learn why we are here in this life. Understanding our purpose and what we are meant to do while we are here will have a significant impact on the choices and decisions we will make from this point forward. The time we devote to reflecting on 1) the lessons attained while enduring challenges, 2) the gifts we will use to carry out our purpose, and 3) the people or places that will be positively impacted as a result of our commitment to carry out our purpose, is the greatest investment we will ever make in our lifetime.

In order to grow and transcend circumstances that no longer serve us, we must be willing to admit and accept responsibility for what has or is occurring in our lives. It's the only way we will be able to alleviate resistance, obstacles, and challenges that prevent us from mentally, physically, emotionally, and spiritually moving toward our desired experience.

Nothing occurs, exists, or shows up in our lives without reason. If *it* is in our life, *it* is there for a reason. We must learn the art of utilization - using everything and every experience that arises in our lives for a greater purpose, no matter how painful or pleasurable. Conflict between a belief (sense of worthiness) and a desire (an intention or requested experience) will manifest in our lives as a challenge, an obstacle, or a path derailed. We must open our minds to comprehending the *fact* that we are responsible for calling into our lives undesired situations and outcomes just the same.

Acquiring knowledge that helps to shed light on aspects of ourselves that no longer serve us, strengthen positive aspects that do serve us, or even change our perceptions of failure and loss, is a monumental step towards creating a reality that is more in alignment with who we really are.

We are only ever choosing one of two *true emotions* in a single moment: that is either love or fear. Now, keep in mind there are a gamut of emotions that exist within the collective (those with whom we are connected, which is essentially everyone), as well as the individual consciousness, that can be described as good or not so good. However, when narrowing down the cause behind *why* an emotion has surfaced, we will find that it is either rooted in love or rooted in fear.

Letting go of the excuses we use to justify shortcomings in our lives begins with acknowledging that we are the only ones responsible for what does or does not occur in our lives This is often times a tough pill to swallow, especially when involving situations that arise seemingly as a result of someone else's poor choices and behaviors. We must begin to recognize that, regardless of the outcome, we are always playing a role in, and contributing to, the creation of whatever we experience. Through the acknowledgement of personal contribution in all experiences - both harmful and helpful – we automatically become empowered to make better choices and decisions that are more conducive to our quest for achievement and fulfillment. Ultimately, taking this approach to life enables us to exemplify respect and compassion for:

- Ourselves
- Everyone involved in a situation or relationship
- Humanity (the entire world)

The beliefs we maintain about ourselves must be in alignment with the possibility that everything we require already exists in order for us to become everything we aspire. Negative beliefs maintained about who we are will oppose the alignment and acquisition of everything we need in order to become and experience everything we desire. Let us take self-inventory and ask: *Will what I think and believe to be true get me to where I am trying to be in life?* If our thoughts and beliefs are in alignment with our destiny, the idea of entertaining any *buts,* excuses, or justifications for shortcomings will cease to exist. Taking ownership of how our lives are unfolding and then gaging the distance between what is true for us *right now* and what is true at our core, are essential steps in respect to increasing our awareness for potential opportunities that lead to growth. Of course, this would absolutely entail changing our beliefs to match our true potential and our greatest aspirations.

Consider it wise that we begin understanding that within the world we live, everyone and everything is connected to everyone and everything else. *Everything* includes the known and the unknown, as well as the seen and the unseen. What this means is that every single one of our thoughts, actions, words, and beliefs not only have an impact on us and our lives, but they also affect everything and everyone else existing within this Universe. We have the amazing opportunity to choose to exist in such a way that everything else around us is *positively* affected by our actions and decisions. Taking on this outlook alone will immediately shift our perception of how things are showing up or occurring in our lives.

We *are* wise. We *are* loved. We *are* bright souls excitedly awaiting the opportunity to shine. We *are already* successful. We *are already* fulfilled. We *are* compassionate beings who are choosing to love ourselves through to the preferred side of our life experience. Whatever we desire already exists. Whatever we desire to be already is. Whatever we need to realize our dreams and aspirations *already exists within us.*

We must remember to always nurture ourselves in this process of learning to alter our current belief systems to ones that are more constructive. Doing our best to refrain from judging ourselves for going where we have gone, being who we have been, or even perceiving our lives, our relationships, and the world in ways that are harmful and discouraging, is something we should constantly strive to achieve. The fact that we each have chosen to read, listen to, and write - yes, I am included in this journey - this book says that something within is urging us to make a different choice.

We should really listen.

The idea that we have come to this awareness should spark some sense of inspiration that will hopefully encourage us to rise higher in our quest to become more of who we truly aspire to be.

Let's be grateful. Some people never arrive to such awareness and spend most of their lives learning how to cope with pain and regret instead of rising above circumstances, brushing off their bottoms, and letting of the *buts* that stand between them and a desired goal. Prior to this moment, we may have previously subscribed to the false reality that what we truly desire will never come into fruition and therefore must settle for a life of mediocrity and emptiness. No longer will this be true, or even possible for us. As a result of our journey together, we will be motivated to make a different choice - a more loving choice. I am here to remind you of the power of decision that lies within.

♥♥♥♥♥

Before moving on to the next chapter, I want to take the time to thoroughly review the principles shared previously about attraction and connectivity, and how it relates to what we may or may not be experiencing in our lives today. To the degree in which we believe in this principle is the degree in which we will be able to create your preferred state of existence. One of the easiest ways to monitor our levels of connectivity, and whether we are prohibiting the flow of possibility, resources, and preferred experiences into our lives, is to reflect on the relationships we have attracted. Remember, *our relationships are mirrors that will always affirm what it is that we believe to be true about ourselves - negatively or positively.* This bit of revelation is extremely important because the relationships we maintain not only indicate what is going on inside of us but can most certainly affect (positive) or infect (negative) us in the pursuit of happiness, freedom, and fulfillment. Our energetic unions with others play a major part in what is or is not allowed into our lives. Our friends, siblings, significant others, co-workers, etc., are either contributing to or depleting us of the love required for us to be, have, or experience more of what we desire.

Listed below are ways in which you can determine whether or not a relationship is clouding your outlook or positively influencing your perspective of what is possible in, for, and through your life.

Relationships that cloud your perspective of love and possibility will:

- reinforce your fears, remind you of past pains, and neglect to support you towards becoming your highest good and greatest potential.

- prevent you from sharing your true feelings about the people, events, and circumstances that arise in your life.

- foster a sense of disbelief, distrust, unworthiness, indecision, fear, frustration, and impatience.

- distract you from or decrease your belief in the potential of connecting with, or attracting into your life, all that is required for achievement and fulfillment.

- perpetuate a sense of abandonment and support the illusion of separateness and aloneness.

- encourage dishonesty within yourself about your lack of alignment with what you truly desire. This means failing to shed light on the fact that your surroundings, relationships, circumstances, choices, thoughts, perceptions, and actions do not match up with what you envision becoming.

- encourage you to maintain a "me versus everyone else" mentality and perspective, which often leads to living in a constant state of victimization.

- neglect to help you understand how past experiences are hindering your ability to transcend recurring circumstances that no longer serve you, especially when your relationship is no longer a positive contribution to your life.

- Encourage you to place blame for painful and discontenting experiences that seemingly show up in your life without reason.

- skew your outlook of abundance through their complaints and constant sharing of what seems to be missing or lacking.

Relationships that enhance your perspective of love and possibility will:

- reinforce your unique abilities, gifts, and talents, as well as

- remind you of your purpose and enthusiastically support you towards becoming your highest good and greatest potential.
- Cooperate in allowing the open space required to share true feelings about the people, events, and circumstances that arise.
- inspire you to maintain the mindset that declares everything within the Universe is connected, and everything you need to be more of who you really are already exists and is waiting for your alignment and allowance.
- encourage you to be accountable for the choices in your life that resulted in painful and discontenting experiences.
- prevent you from allowing negative thoughts to prevail in your mind when faced with trials and tribulation. Foster a sense of belief, worthiness, patience, love, connection, and happiness.
- remind, confirm, and affirm your belief in the potential of connecting with, or attracting into your life, all that is required for achievement and fulfillment.
- perpetuate a sense of security and comfort, and remind you that being alone is a choice, not a punishment.
- encourage you to remain mindful of the relationships you maintain and determine whether or not the people who surround you support you in creating the life you prefer.
- encourage honesty within yourself about the lack of alignment. This means shedding light on the fact that your surroundings, relationships, circumstances, choices, thoughts, perceptions, and actions do not match with what you envision becoming.

Overcoming challenges and obstacles starts with understanding that we have the potential to attract or connect with everything we need for success and fulfillment, even despite the *buts* we've accumulated throughout our lives. To delve deeper into the topic of awareness, I would encourage you to reflect on the following:

- Always be willing to acknowledge and honor the significance of others in your life. Releasing judgment about who they are, or are not, creates space within you to invite into your life exactly what you need to transcend current circumstances. You can otherwise place more time into focusing on what you are becoming instead of on what is not occurring. You also become empowered to concentrate more on investing into yourself and heightening your awareness of what is possible for your life, rather than focusing on the actions of others that are impossible to control to begin with.

- Recognize the power and value in connections and relationships, and how they broaden your perspective of what is possible, or not.

- Practice asking yourself, others, the Universe, the Creator, etc., for *exactly* what you want and desire, and then align your thoughts, actions, and conversations to reflect that it is as if what you require has already arrived.

- Develop the art of connection and remain constant in your effort to consciously exist, request, confirm, accept, and choose healthy and positive relationships and circumstances.

- Honor yourself enough to set boundaries that will minimize the experience of false and negative connections that will derail you from having, being, and doing what it is you desire with and in your life.

To accomplish this, you need to be extremely clear about what is or is not missing, about what no longer serves you, about what you need, about what requires healing, and lastly, clear in your request for others to honor and respect the intentions you have set for yourself.

Use your relationships to gage where you are in your quest for "more" or "better." Trust that they are present to empower you to see what is missing, what needs work, and what needs healing. You'd be surprised how a shift in perspective and the removal of judgment will help you to develop a more constructive perspective of how things occur and what is possible for you. You can grow more aware by being mindful of how and to whom you offer invitations.

Invite people into your life or connect with people who are willing to understand and support where you are and where you are trying to go - who you are now, and who you are trying to become.

Invite people into your life or connect with people who mirror your positive and constructive ideas and perspectives, and then honor your uniqueness while doing so.

Invite people into your life or connect with people who will stand in support of healing the "hole" for the sake of obtaining wholeness through the reparation of past pains, hurt feelings, abandonment, and neglect.

Invite people into your life or connect with people who are committed to helping you see things as they are and not what you want or wanted them to be.

Invite people into your life or connect with people who will tell you the truth, no matter the outcome, and even if it hurts.

Only accept the invitations of entering and connecting to the life of another person if you are willing to make the same positive and constructive contributions towards their growth and evolution.

Learn to rely on the intangible aspects of this Universe that can also serve as resources or relationships to help you reach desired outcomes. A good example would be to invite the spirits of your ancestors who have come before you and managed to reach success, overcome challenges, and surmount pain and misfortune. Another would be to trust in the power of connecting yourself with the energy of those who are already succeeding and flourishing in ways you envision doing so in your own life.

Sowing Seeds (Choices)

"Seeds of faith are always within us; sometimes it takes a crisis to nourish and encourage their growth."

- Susan L Taylor

Two important goals we can all strive to achieve in endeavor to love ourselves more fully, and ultimately, *let go of your buts* are 1) having a clear understanding of *your* definition of success, and 2) being fully aware of how *you* will *measure* the attainment of such success on a daily, weekly, monthly, or annual basis. Keep in mind, I am not just referring to success that pertains to the acquisition external things that have nothing at all to do with who you *really* are. Trinkets, toys, houses, cars, money, or even statuses and labels, are things we consume in celebration of success and achievement, but they don't necessarily qualify as attainment on a deeper level that far surpasses materialism. I am encouraging you to discover what success means *for* you, as well as what it means *to* you. This means having a clear definition of what success beyond the attainment of a thing or an object means for you and then being able to determine what your life would amount to if you were unable to complete the goals required for such attainment.

Need I remind you: the purpose of our lives stretches far beyond self-gratification. Therefore, when considering what our lives may amount to once we reach success, we can aim to think along the lines of contribution and legacy. So, not only should we be able to define success for our respective lives, we should also be able to describe what it looks like and how it will feel to us in the moment of attainment. Once this is accomplished, we can then take our consideration one step further and estimate how the outcome of our success will positively affect the lives of those around us. Through the deliberate use of imagination, coupled with the ability to tap into the emotions that arise because of contemplation, we become empowered to hone in on precisely how it will feel to experientially live out our dreams and aspirations. As mentioned in previous chapters, if we ever find ourselves completely off course with our goals and aspirations, we can use positive feelings centered on the fruition of future success, achievement, and contribution to navigate our way back into alignment. The bottom line is this, mapping out how we get from where we are now to where we would like to be is done in accordance with how we *define* and what we *feel* about success.

We must grow more mindful about whether we are striving for achievement based on what society portrays as success. It is easy to get tricked into comparing our lives to those we see played out on social media platforms, television programming, magazines, etc. When doing this, we can potentially become fixated on attempting to consume and accumulate the things we *think we want* just to prove and demonstrate success. Yet, when we are alone in solitude, quietly conceding to the yearning of our souls, we can most likely hear the calling of our lives echoing in the emptiness of our hearts. We must begin listening to, and trusting in the small, whispered voice of *intuition* we hear when we take the time to assess where we are in our individual journeys. When honest, we find ourselves harboring shame or guilt for having attested to an idea of perfection and fulfillment that is truly an illusion when compared to what we have been assigned to bring into completion in our own lives. Nestled deep in the center of every one of us lies the wisdom that constantly nudges and reminds us that success can only be mastered when we do away with following society's cookie-cutter patterns and definitions of success. The journey of a fulfilled life begins with the choice to express ourselves lovingly and authentically - so much so that carving out our own unique path to success becomes inevitable.

One thing is for certain, however, and that is, if we continue to follow what everyone in society has defined as successful, we will forever remain lost in the cyclical chase of something that doesn't really exist or will leave us feeling disheartened and incomplete when the race is finally over. Hopping off this hamster wheel of emptiness starts with creating a relationship with our intuition. Intuition is especially useful when attempting to make monumental decisions, or transition from one circumstance to another. Our intuition compels us to stop, listen, act, or retreat so that we may receive information and/or guidance from a realm beyond our mental comprehension. Continuing to have those quiet conversations (through meditation, nature walks, prayer, sitting still, journaling, etc.) with ourselves helps us to associate our feelings and emotions with what we define as true success. We must continue our efforts to gain clarity on what would leave us feeling as though we have made some degree of contribution to this world beyond the attainment of things that promote self-gratification. Once we are able to maintain this type of clarity, we can then set an intention to really minimize societal chatter and focus on carving out pathways that enable us to love ourselves into full potential.

It is true that some of the aspects of success we envision may entail the attainment of a career, a loving relationship, a new home, financial independence, or maybe even children. Yet, getting to know who we *really* are, versus who we are currently being, is an essential step to take towards reaching fulfillment in our lives. The next would be to determine what we are doing or not doing as we aim to create what we desire and prefer. Recognizing how things may or may not be unfolding, occurring, and recurring is useful in determining specific actions, behaviors, patterns, and routines that require modification. On the other hand, rather than placing so much emphasis on observing the *actions* that perpetuate failure, we can also consider who we are *being* while we are *doing* or *not doing* whatever led us to or away from the path of achieving success as we've defined it. In some cases, it may not even be *what we* are doing, but rather *who we are being* while we are engaged in the *doing* that is affecting progress in our lives. A great place to look is the degree of authenticity, honesty, and vulnerability that we are exhibiting in our intention to experience improvement in our lives.

Being aware of who you need to become in order to flourish in your pursuit of success is vital. If you are still oblivious to the shifts that may be required of your personality, mindset, outlook, or attitude in order to attain the success you desire, set some time aside to truly take inventory of how you are feeling about who you are being. Once you have done so, make a conscious effort to determine whether who you are being today (inclusive of desires, skills, knowledge, experience, and will to thrive) is the person you need to be in order to reach your desired state or outcome. Compare the "who and how you are being today" with the person you envision as being successful. Take note of the variance and set the intention of adjusting how you think, speak, and act. Once you can mindfully step into the gap between the two versions of who you are and what you are meant to become, the next step will be to give yourself permission to do the following:

- Love yourself *exactly* as you are now.
- Get re-acquainted with who you really are at your core.
- Allow the most authentic aspects of you breathe, flourish, and shine despite the pain, rejection, shame, or guilt you harbor.
- Move through and rise above fear to the best of your ability.
- Thrive. Live in the moment. Fail boldly, without apology or shame, knowing that a lesson is being learned along the way.
- Measure your level of integrity, love, happiness, peace, and freedom daily, until it becomes your most natural way of being,
- Trust that integrity, love, happiness, peace, and freedom will always lead you in the *right direction* (for you, not everyone else).
- Trust your intuition enough to act without hesitation, knowing that if you remain in alignment with your truth, you will gain everything you need.
- Know without a doubt that no choice is ever a wrong choice. All choices lead to opportunities to make another choice that

is more in accordance with what you prefer and desire.
- Increase your self-esteem by making and meeting your daily commitments.
- Set realistic goals and make new habits that are in alignment with who you really are.
- Remain humble, yet celebrate with gratitude every growth spurt you make.

Know that striving to do the aforementioned steps on a daily basis costs us absolutely nothing yet puts us in position to gain or experience all that we desire. We are worthy of digging deeper in order to discover the hidden treasures within that make us unique and gifted - qualities that make us wonderfully designed to bring to pass everything that is meant to be carried out in our lives. Discovering the gems dwelling at our core is vital, being that they are the aspects of who we are that will empower us to experience life in a much greater capacity than we may have ever envisioned. Getting to know who we are is a significant step to take towards letting go of outcomes and expectations that may be blinding us of our true potential. *Letting go of* everything that no longer serves us (such as *buts*, excuses, past pains, mistakes, failures, limiting perspectives, negative attitudes, destructive behaviors, etc.) allows us to see clearly, as well as, provides room for the God of your understanding to fulfill His/Her promise - the promise that whatever is meant *for us* to experience, and everything required *for us* to thrive already exists. By letting go of the weighty, unloving thoughts, patterns, beliefs, and conditions that prevent us from receiving or connecting with what is already ours, we are able to become our true selves.

Again, the person you envision becoming and everything that is required for you to experience what you truly desire *already exists*. To analyze *how* you will step towards your desired experiences is not always necessary; however, it starts with *knowing* – more than just believing – the truth behind this principle. There is nothing in this great Universe that hasn't already been created, contemplated, considered, or experienced. Believing that there is more, greater, and better for you to have and be in this lifetime is enough to propel you into discovering and creating all that resides within you - beneath the pain, shame, or sentiments of failure. Dwelling inside of you is *the* magical Creator who has the ability to call forth preferred outcomes and experiences, even in the face of contrasting circumstances.

At any point in our perspective journeys, we can decide to set aside what we know, or what we think we know, in order to allow our true potential to link with all that is possible. This step is vital as it aligns us with the resources and relationships that will elevate us into higher and higher levels of success and fulfillment. The higher we rise, the better we feel. The higher we rise, the more confident we become. The higher we rise, the more trusting in the possibilities available to us. The higher we rise, the more we understand that the road to success involves more than setting high-targeted goals and milestones in our professional and personal lives. Success and achievement entail more than identifying the correct amount of effort to be applied with the right amount of trajectory that will launch us toward a designated objective. The journey to success starts with loving ourselves exactly as we are, understanding our true potential, and then opening ourselves up enough to *believe* that all things are possible. C.S. Lewis stated perfectly: "If we find ourselves with a desire that nothing in this world can satisfy, the most probable explanation is that we were made for another world."

Gaining perspective about who we really are and what is truly possible for us won't happen in an instant. Thus, there is no need to be hard on ourselves if the answers to internal queries do not reveal themselves right away. Let us be patient and trusting at the same time. While doing so, we can take a moment to reflect over areas in our lives where we achieved success, without disregarding or judging them based on size, significance, or impact. Understand this: success is success no matter the degree of difficulty, time, or magnitude in which it was fulfilled. The same amount of energy it takes to get up and make our way to work every day is the same amount of energy it will take to remain focused until a desired outcome is reached. The difference lies in *knowing* who we really are and what is truly possible for us based on what we *believe* about ourselves.

Without even being conscious of our actions, we have managed to bring ideas that were once imagined into our physical experience on several occasions throughout our lives. We wouldn't be where we are if we hadn't done so. With this in mind, we can now choose to consciously bring into existence what we desire by believing that what is meant for us already exists. We have unconsciously proven this time and time again. We have proven that success doesn't always *start* with doing something or taking action. It all starts with our perspectives and the thoughts we hold about what is possible. Yes, "faking it until making it" is part what it takes to overcome shortcomings that prohibit success. However, often times these types of deeds are unfeasible without first adjusting limiting mindsets and perspectives to ones that are emitted from positive and healthy aspects of who we really are.

Dreams that seem unrealistic, or impossible, are just as attainable as those we have already achieved. Often, peers, teachers, parents, and other influential people we encounter attempt to minimize our potential for disappointment by insisting that we be *realistic* with your *goals and expectations*. The concept of living in reality is one thing. The ability to create our own reality is an entirely different, more empowering perspective by which to live. One thing people who play it safe by being realistic with their lives have in common is the negligence in understanding that some dreamers actually become doers. Most doers did not become doers without first dreaming. Therefore, all ideas, concepts, and inventions that have come to fruition since the beginning of time were at some point unrealistic.

When we bring our own respective lives into this conversation, we can begin to recognize how it only took one thought to alter choices, decisions, actions, and behaviors so that they matched up and led us toward our desired outcome - no matter how unrealistic it seemed. All ideas and thoughts have the potential to become reality as long as we keep our minds resolute about realizing it.

The idea here is to compel us to move toward being *unrealistic* with our potential and ability to succeed. Do not mistake this with being blind and careless with our desires. I am speaking of being unrealistic in a sense of becoming obliged to exceed our current circumstances and mindsets. Understand this: to be realistic is to be more of what we *already are.* To be *unrealistic* is to tap into the side of *who we really are* that has yet to be realized in this physical realm. Unrealistic ideas are usually birthed from this untapped facet of our true selves. Recognize that far-fetched ideas, thoughts, and beliefs stem from our souls' determination to live out experientially exactly what it desires.

Allow me to reiterate: who you really are and what you truly desire already exists. Simply practice tapping into *the highest version of who you really are inside.* Doing so enables you to bring everything *she* desires into fruition by way of faith, focus, imagination, and will. Thus, your daily assignment now includes becoming purer with your intentions to complete the following:

1. View the things, people, and circumstances that transpire in your life through the lens of love, compassion, and positivity - don't forget to include yourself.

2. Be open to meeting people and creating circumstances that support the fruition of your desired results. Release people and circumstances that no longer serve you as soon as you possibly can. Do your best to do this without resistance or judgment about who they are and what occurred as a result

of allowing their presence in your life.

3. Align patterns, behaviors, and actions so that they support achievement and attainment of everything you desire to be, have, and experience in life.

I encourage you to *compete upward* (with your true self that is waiting to come forth through you, rather than with people and circumstances that do not define who you really are), evaluate your choices, correct injurious actions, and set goals that are clear, concise, and measurable. Avoid losing sight of the intention to generate new thought patterns and belief systems that will completely change how you experience the world and what happens around you. Recognize the hidden aspects of yourself that prohibit you from being or becoming *more of who you really are* beyond your talent, professional skills, level of education, or financial status. At the end of the day, you have the power to ensure a lifetime (not just momentary experiences) of success through your ability to operate at newer and higher levels of potential that exceed anything you previously imagined.

Below are four terms (three of which are followed by a dictionary definition) that are vital to your journey of evolution and aspiration to love yourself to full potential. It is wise to truly retain the meaning behind each term so that you may understand exactly how the terms you use and the references you make can negatively or positively affect the fruition of your goals and aspirations.

1. **Success** – *the achievement of something desired, planned, or attempted; the gaining of fame or prosperity.*

2. **Excuses** – *an explanation offered as a reason for being excused; a plea offered in extenuation of a fault or for release from an obligation, promise, etc.*

3. **But** – *on the contrary; contrary to exception; yet*

4. **Self-Actualization:**

    (Define this term by describing "success" in your own words. Be sure to include the purest, most honest depiction of who you will become should you reach your highest potential. Leave nothing out.)

Notice that there was no dictionary definition provided for the fourth term in this list. This is done purposefully so that you may not only define the term on your own, but so that you may also keep a written definition in this book in the event you need to refer to it later as you continue embarking on the path of *letting go of your buts*, excuses, justifications, and rationalizations. It would also be wise to write your definitions for both success and self-realization on a Post-It and stick it somewhere highly visible.

In order to begin to understand what it means for you to reach success and self-actualization, I have provided a list of questions for you to answer. As you complete the tenth question, you will begin to recognize the common thread woven throughout your compilation of responses. The pattern may not be obvious initially but continue to process and digest your answers until you are able to clearly see the commonality. Once you can recognize the pattern in your responses, you will be able to clearly define what success and self-realization means *for you*.

1. What aspects of life make you ache when you contemplate painful experiences in your past, or that you may wish to heal in the lives of others?

2. What do you most often daydream about?

3. Who do you envision yourself becoming?

4. How do you want to feel about your future?
    - Consider the choices and decisions you have made in respect to your life, body, relationships, career, spiritual life, or education. Then, consider the vision you have in your heart and mind.
    - Are the choices you've made, and are making, leading in the *right direction?*
    - How do you feel about where you are currently?

5. What would you want others to write about you once you have achieved everything you set out to accomplish?

6. What legacy do you wish to leave behind?

7. What impact in the lives of others, or the world at large, would you want associated with your name?

8. What do you yearn to see as a result of the impact your work has had or will continue to have on the world?

9. What do you see as your best contribution to humanity?

10. Describe in three words how you will feel if you were to accomplish or everything listed above.
    - This step is key. To constantly remind yourself of this feeling, as well as recognizing the current contrast of what you may be feeling in any given moment is what will keep you on course to dream fruition.

Setting the Stage

"It's not the will to win that matters, it's the will to prepare to win that is most important."

- Michael Jordan

Here are a few habits I would like to encourage each of us to avoid making whenever we find ourselves discouraged during tough times: quitting or leaving what we started unfinished; changing target dates and deadlines, or modifying goals and milestones in ways that derail, rather than further, your quest for achievement. *These habits are easy to cultivate, yet we should refrain from making them our first options to consider in our attempt to avoid failure.* Trust me, I completely understand that the road to success requires the traveler to be agile in their progression. It's no secret that the path to achievement may often compel us to be simultaneously vigilant in our commitment, as well as flexible in our approach to overcoming challenges and obstacles. Adaptability is most certainly the precursor for attempting to endeavor a road less traveled; however, let's always be mindful of the ease and convenience of *relying* on adaptability to keep us in "the game." When we are truthful about this habit, we will often find that all we are really doing is spinning a web of procrastination, which is most certainly out of alignment with loving ourselves. Changing an end game works for most because it enables us to downsize effort when we become overwhelmed and discouraged by the inundation of tasks and activities that need to be completed in order to meet our goals and aspirations. It also helps to increase excitement and feasibility, or temporarily boost our egos high enough to "get back on track." Yet, once we can step back and get a wider view of what actually got accomplished each time we trimmed our goals, we will recognize that we aren't even in the vicinity of what we initially set out to accomplish. The damage to our self-esteem upon this awareness can be debilitating. Thus, instead of moving the finish line forward, cutting corners, or scaling down our visions, we can try recalculating the amount of time, effort, and resources it will take to help us reach our goals. Keep in mind that the idea is to complete this task sooner rather than later. All the more reason why it is at the beginning of our endeavor when we must be willing to: analyze our potential, be mindful of our beliefs, and have clarity in our definition of success.

Whether our goals are to change careers, lose weight, produce music, start a business, get married, buy a house, or simply complete a project that was started, preparation for our venture toward fruition is essential. As we are learning to be more mindful of our thoughts, beliefs, and actions, we as women must recognize our tendency to make impulsive decisions and choices based on our emotions, as well as on how something or someone has made us feel. This realization should not be taken as a judgment or negative criticism. I merely bring this up so that we are empowered to channel our energies and emotions more constructively. The objective here is to grow more aware of our capacity to create our own realities and attract into our lives the resources required for us to reach our full potential. Emotion and passion are essential to this process, as they serve as the guiding forces that move us along, or away from, our quest for accomplishment. Often times, they are the sparks that ignite the motivation necessary to stay the course and persevere through tough times. Yet, they are also the catalysts for disappointment and discouragement when things don't quite work out the way we expected. To avoid this, it is wise for us to stop, check in with how we are feeling, assess what we are thinking about how we are feeling, and then select a path or action that is conducive for healing and productivity. We must learn to invest the time it takes to truly prepare and evaluate the road ahead as it relates to our true potential and ability for accomplishment. *We are the only ones capable of dictating what is, or is not, achievable in our lives. We are the only ones who can measure our capacity to be or become all that is required to attain every single outcome we desire.* Taking some time to prepare, or possibly even research, exactly what it will take for us to reach the end line is always our best option and it minimizes the need to adjust timelines and milestones. Especially when we are endeavoring a notable undertaking, preparation helps us to recognize and assess (sooner than later) whether or not the road to success is going to be more challenging than we previously envisioned.

Let's go back to what was discussed earlier about having the inclination to be *unrealistic* with our dreams and aspirations. *Preparation* is vital in our ability to accomplish goals that may seem impossible or unfathomable to the mind. I am not just speaking about sharpening skills through education and training, which are also prerequisites to growing secure enough in our abilities to complete the necessary tasks to make certain milestones in our endeavors. I am speaking about being environmentally (maintaining mindfulness of people, places, and things that surround us), mentally (focusing on thoughts and perceptions that promote success), spiritually (aligning with the creation of abundance, money, resources, and relationships that support growth and fruition), emotionally (expressing everything in a way that generates goodness and love), and physically (maintaining health and wellness) prepared enough to obliterate perceived limitations and reach our full potential as envisioned in our hearts and minds. Preparation in this context is all encompassing of what, who, and how we need to be, think, act, perceive, and believe as we make our way toward success. This expanded perspective of what it means to be prepared is exactly what will enable us to keep the bar of possibility raised as we push ourselves beyond perceived limitations to become everything we envision, or even more.

If we were to take a second to consider the concept of having a dream or aspiration, we will recognize that *reality* ceases to exist the moment the vision is conceived. Remember, all thoughts and ideas are created solely from the perceptions and feelings we hold - all of which provide no physical or tangible evidence of existence. There is nothing *real* about a dream or vision until we make it so. To be *realistic* about what we think, believe, and perceive only supports our ability to create more of the same of what we currently see, learn, and experience. With this understanding, we may as well remove all perceived restrictions and limitations and shoot for the stars in respect to creating exactly what we desire. Again, preparation supports our ability to keep dreams and aspirations elevated without wavering. To maintain the course to fruition, to rise above average and mediocrity, it is imperative that we remain *unrealistic* in our current abilities.

This simply means that we must practice being mindful of the places, situations, circumstances, and relationships that either support or distract us from our ambitions. We must be willing to making necessary adjustments so that who we are, who we allow in our lives, and where we happen to be in any given moment, line up with what we want to achieve, have, be, or experience. As we recognize that our lives do not have to be perfect for us to experience life as wonderful, we can still be accountable for creating one that is balanced enough to allow options and opportunities for growth and change to continuously present themselves. We are responsible for creating that space of invitation.

To mentally prepare for growth, transition, and ultimately success, we must be willing to face all of our fears (the root cause of our perceived limitations), or at least those we feel will prohibit us from moving into our next level of success and fulfillment. One by one, we can take on our fears by listing every possible way a challenge can be resolved resultantly. We can weigh the possibilities of conquest against the worst outcome that could possibly arise as a result of confronting our fears. Nine times out of ten, we will discover that the idea of the fear is actually much greater than the actual act of conquering them. We must commit to practicing this until every one of our fears begins to dissipate.

We shouldn't be too alarmed in the event we discover the need to undergo a mental makeover that will support our ability to break bad habits that are currently limiting our potential to be more of who we really are. The key to unlock any gate that blocks our path to success is to start our endeavor with positive thoughts – even before we take a single step. Sometimes reaching a desired state or outcome entails embarking upon a complete overhaul or lifestyle change rather than a series of quick fixes or shortcuts. Once we make the decision to transition from one phase of existence to the next, having a more constructive perspective becomes imperative. Otherwise, we make ourselves susceptible to being victimized and demeaned by our own negative self-talk when things do not go according to plan. Positioning ourselves to maintain focus also entails understanding the *why* of our goals and desires, as opposed to the *how* (the road to fruition and how it will appear) or the *what* (the end result). It may also entail making investments in coaching, training, or consultants to help guide and motivate us whenever we face potential sabotage or derailment. More important than anything else, we must love ourselves into believing in our ability to reach desired states or experiences.

Spiritual preparation is one facet of success that is often overlooked, yet embracing the process of becoming conscious of our inner true self is the difference between achieving a goal and reaching full potential. Alignment with our soul-selves is to raise our level of consciousness beyond the ordinary existence and awakening to the passion, purpose, and truth that may be lying dormant within. It means going beyond the mind and the ego and realizing who we really are. Spiritual preparation paves way for harmony and attraction, and also sets the stage for a life free of tension, fear, and anxiety - all of which perpetuate distraction and resistance along the path to fruition.

Financial preparation can stand in a category of its own, especially as it relates to saving, establishing credit, fundraising, or clearing debts, all of which can greatly position us for the achievement of what we truly desire to have, be, or experience. However, I am more inclined to speak about the management of money in the space between spiritual and emotional preparation. Meaning, our ability to be spiritually aligned with attracting and allowing abundance into our lives is directly reflective of how we feel about attaining it. Depending on whether we harbor a lack-minded, or affluence-minded, perspective about money and wealth, we can destroy, disallow, create, and/or receive into our lives all that is required for us to experience the life we desire. This means, that being financially prepared also entails maintaining the mindset of abundance in such a way that the Universe has no choice but to support us in bringing increases into our reality. It entails perceiving of a journey toward our desired outcome and arriving to fruition in spite of our circumstances or the state of an economy. It's truly knowing that financial abundance is our birthright and an aspect of life of which we are truly deserving.

Emotional preparation entails everything I mentioned in previous chapters that speaks to being fully aware of our feelings. It's no secret that the greatest challenge in the pursuit of fulfillment, especially for women, is to create synergy among the varying emotions that arise in our day-to-day comings and goings. Yet, the more we are able to remain balanced and in control of our emotions, the more enabled we are to stretch beyond the momentary tendencies toward reactive behaviors and, instead, remain conscious about making choices and decisions that positively affect our lives, our relationships, and our environments. Emotional mindfulness takes practice. It's more than maintaining the ability to recognize and express negative feelings that cloud our perspectives and beliefs, or positive feelings that generate a sense of gratitude. Understand that it is also about allowing ourselves to feel (rather than ignore or resist) whatever we may be experiencing and then measuring the truth about what we are believing because of our feelings. Adjusting in what we believe to be true about what we are experiencing, consequent to being mindful of our feelings, enables us to decide or choose our next action in ways that are healthy and loving rather than destructive.

Maintaining good health and wellness rounds out the process of preparing for the reception of everything required for us to have, be, and experience desired outcomes and aspirations in full capacity. Physically positioning ourselves for success and fulfillment entails choosing, acting, and being in ways that lead to love, peace, and happiness, not just in our lives, but also in the lives of those who surround us. Being physically active or exercising regularly, eating healthy, getting plenty of rest, minimizing stress, and maintaining loving relationships are also extremely vital to how far we will travel along the journey of fruition. We should continuously aim to keep in mind just how much poor physical health can lead to poor mental health, and vice versa. Nurturing our physical health does not just entail our bodies, but our minds and spirits as well. Regardless of our choice to be mindful or inattentive, all three aspects of our existence remain connected and any one of them can have positive or adverse effects upon the other. The intention behind our endeavor to maintain good health and heal our bodies is to ensure that our self-esteem remains high no matter where we go, who we meet, or what life may bring. The better we feel about ourselves inside and out, the further we will travel in our pursuit of becoming more of who we really are. The healthier we are, the more likely we are to avail ourselves to relationships, experiences, and circumstances that promote elevation and evolution in our lives.

♥♥♥♥♥

Understand that there is a difference between sharing what is real for us right now, in this current moment, and what we may perceive to be realistic for our lives. Do not *ever* be afraid to tell the truth about what is real for you in this moment, no matter how good, or not so good, it may sound to others. We must strive to do our very best not to confuse our interpretations that define the stories we tell about what happens with the truth. Sticking with the facts is much more productive than sharing an inflated "story" just to gain the attention and sympathy of others who may not even have the wherewithal, concern, or capacity to help us. Rehashing an over-exaggerated account of an uncomfortable encounter or event only keeps us stuck in the cycle of recreating what we momentarily despise. Remaining focused on the truth ushers in the opportunity and awareness for growth and transition much sooner than later. It is impossible to move into higher levels of potential without first acknowledging and being accountable for what is currently occurring in our lives. To be utterly honest and authentic about how we are behaving, thinking, speaking, sharing, and choosing *now* helps with creating goals and milestones that are achievable in our *tomorrow*. Rather than entertaining a lack-minded perspective, authenticity generates plenty of room for allowing who we are not and what we don't have to evolve or emerge. It creates the space for us to remove limitations and expand our point of view so that we may see and perceive of possibilities that were previously inconceivable.

On the opposite side of the coin, thinking we are or have more than we really have is dangerous and misleading. Having a false or inflated perspective about what is or is not occurring makes the potential for failure a greater possibility. Again, remaining honest and humble, especially when life begins to feel cumbersome and bleak, is our best approach. Rather than letting our current reality dissuade or discourage us, we can aim to recognize and understand right here, right now, that the path to success just may be 3, 5, 7, or even 10 times harder than we imagined. Thus, we can *prepare* accordingly. Having a clear perspective of who we are and the truest measure of our potential and capabilities helps when it comes time to planning our approach to success and fulfillment. We become more empowered to figure out how to increase effort and sustainability by way of joining forces with others who have the resources we require. At the same time, we can begin investing time towards discovering ways to enhance our own knowledge domain. We can surround ourselves with people who have already accomplished *unrealistic* feats and are excited about supporting us as we venture along our own lanes of triumph.

Being prepared and having a true assessment of what it takes to realize our goals, ambitions, and desires makes it ten times less likely that we will allow excuses and justifications to rationalize our shortcomings. We can also grow more mindful through research, as well as learning from the mistakes others have made, so that we are less likely to run into the same pitfalls and disappointments as a result of not being properly equipped. Being prepared keeps us ahead in the game. Correctly assessing the *right* amount of effort, time, and resources needed helps with developing persistence and perseverance. It also supports our proclivity for maintaining a focus on what *is working* and *what's possible,* rather than what is going wrong.

As we continue the practice of releasing our *buts*, I would suggest that we remain mindful of this one fact: no one ever said the success and fulfillment we desire was going to be easily realized. This is not to say that instantaneous fruition is not possible. After all, the objective of all that I have shared thus far is to encourage us to begin aligning all of our thoughts, beliefs, actions, and conversations in accordance with preferred experiences and outcomes. When this occurs, all things are possible. Still, very seldom can an idea or desire come to fruition in the moment of conception. Thus, patience is highly recommended, if not required. Keeping this notion in the forefront of our minds makes it very hard to perceive our vision as unattainable. The degree in which we are able to bring an aspiration into fruition occurs at the level in which we believe in our ability to have or experience it.

Your Journey Begins Here

"I am not losing. I am still here. I am still fighting. When you die, it doesn't mean you lose {to cancer...you beat {cancer} by how you live, why you live and in the manner in which you live."

- Stuart Scott

*W*henever taking the time to sit down and truly contemplate where we are, as well as who we have become as women, we may discover that we have reached a point in our lives where we've either stopped listening to ourselves, lost touch with who we really are on the inside or have completely forgotten what makes us and our lives extraordinary. It is within moments of reflection where reconnecting with ourselves, our goals, and what makes us happy, helps with maintaining alignment with our passion and purpose, as well as striving to live at our highest level of potential and self-love. Many of us are guilty of not only losing ourselves in the pursuit of happiness and fulfillment by way of our relationships, families, careers, etc., but we also tend to lose sight of the true reason behind why we are here to begin with. This occurs consequent to the unconscious decision to place significance and meaning on everything, and everyone, other than ourselves. Thus, the power to push beyond boundaries and limitations gets weakened with each disappointment or shortcoming we experience when desires and aspirations fail to transpire as we envision. The result: our ability to maintain healthy, supportive and authentic relationships with ourselves becomes almost unrecognizable.

Let's take a moment to ascertain where you are on your individual path. Let's suppose you are a woman who embraces courage and your *buts* have nothing to do with overcoming fears. *Maybe* you are tired of being "sick and tired" of *experiencing lack* in your life and are ready to pursue avenues that will generate abundance and prosperity. *Maybe* you are a professional who has achieved the highest level of success in your career and the time for transition has reached you much sooner than you were prepared. *Maybe* you're simply exhausted from watching life pass you by without any clear understanding as to how to make the most of whatever time in your life remains. *Maybe* you are ready to harness your internal power to create exactly what you desire to experience in your relationships, your environments, your career or your business, but are clueless as to where to begin. *Maybe* you are experiencing boredom with your current circumstances and the yearning for rejuvenation has grown quite cumbersome. Or, *maybe* you have this brilliant idea nestled inside your heart and seeing as you have all these other roles to uphold – mother, daughter, head of the household, provider, employee, etc. – you can't quite find the motivation you need to see your dreams through to fruition.

Obviously, there are a plethora of *maybes* that could potentially describe where you happen to be in your life, in this current moment. Despite whatever your situation may be and whatever challenges you may be facing, understand that riding the wave of self-love is an important component to living well and maintaining harmony in your life. Preserving a state of gratitude or appreciation for where you are and who you have become makes it easier to accept, rather than hide or suppress, both your weaknesses and strengths. Self-love compels you to have compassion for yourself as you struggle to discover purpose, value and meaning in your life. It helps with distinguishing the variance between your needs and your wants, your stories and your truths. Forgiving yourself and making peace with all your shortcomings opens the pathway that will lead you to the fulfillment of your greatest aspirations.

Hopefully after reading all that has been shared thus far in this book, you are beginning to contemplate your thoughts, desires, dreams, or visions, as well as the relationships, circumstances, environments, professional endeavors, and your overall life in a new, more empowering light. We are always arriving to exactly where we are because of the situations we encounter, and the choices and decisions we make throughout. Clearly, our wants and desires will continue to change or evolve, but what remains the same is the opportunity to make new choices and decisions that are in alignment with our truth.

Now, with that said, here's something for each of us to consider: *if we can begin to trust that our deepest desires and aspirations do not reside in our hearts without reason, we empower ourselves to resist perceiving the people, events and circumstances that arise in our lives as "wrong" or "bad," instead of purposeful, healthy, or required as preparation for something in our future.* We can opt to stop fighting against who we really are by hoping, thinking and desiring situations and relationships to be different than what they are. We can begin to surrender to the notion that our plans may prove to be something altogether different from the deepest intentions of our souls. We can also begin to recognize contrast, which shows up by way of the anger, frustration, or disappointment experienced when things do not work out as planned, as the very motivation we need to create our preferred outcomes.

Many times, we find ourselves at the crossroads of reflection and regret, only to discover that we have wound up somewhere other than where we desire to be or have become someone other than who we wish to be. When we make it up in our minds not to stay in the state of confusion and stagnation, we can begin to understand that everything that has happened, is happening, and will happen according to how we treat, perceive, and feel about ourselves. Whatever the reason may be that compelled us to pick up or listen to this book, it is my belief that our connection is not some outlandish coincidence, randomly occurring within the scheme of our existence. Remember, the Universe is always at work under the dynamic command of "ask and you shall receive." Or, in an academic analogy, "when the student is ready, the teacher will come." Of all the chapters we've covered thus far, this may be one of the most monumental, as it reminds us to begin the pursuit of change exactly where we are. Not somewhere in the future where we wish to be, or not somewhere in the past where we've already been. We must strive to grow mindful of the various self-loving mindsets and perspectives that we are required to maintain, or practice maintaining, in order for us to prepare for transition in our lives. Besides committing to the choice to create our greatest desires, making the decision to begin, or begin again, right here, right now, is the best thing we can do for ourselves.

Again, it is no twist of fate we have crossed paths. Trust that we are here sharing this moment as a result of reaching some sort of turning point in our lives - hopefully for the better. It's even likely that striving to break the monotony of doing the same mundane tasks day after day after day after day…and halfway expecting a different result has become exhausting.

Attempting to execute practices and rituals required to overcome bad habits that hinder achievement or fulfillment is futile if we first do not get to the root of why we think, believe, perceive, speak and act in ways that are completely out of alignment with our truth and innermost desires. Hopefully we are coming to understand that the underlying cause of poor choices and decisions that lead to shame, guilt, or regret is the lack of love. Our lack of self-awareness and accountability, which prohibits growth and evolution, is exactly why certain people, circumstances and environments look so familiar, or continue to recur in our lives - even when we feel we have made changes in our choices and behaviors. We are incapable of being and having anything we are truly meant to become and experience if we don't first love ourselves - right where we are. If we neglect to love and accept ourselves, we cripple our ability to create preferred experiences, and thus continue to reflect in our lives and relationships everything that has yet to be healed.

I penned this entire series with the ambition of shedding light on, and also healing, the aggrieved aspects of our lives that hold us back from achievement. Deepak Chopra says, "There is only one secret of healing…and it is enlightenment. Enlightenment means going beyond your ego encapsulated identity and realizing that you are the Universe manifesting through a human nervous system and becoming self-aware." Many of the *buts* with which we decorate our conversations centered on desires and aspirations are derivatives of traumatic events experienced in the past. Much like bodily discomfort or injuries need healing before we can move forward or continue with exercise or physical activity that ensures good health, we must be accountable for healing the emotional wounds resultant of previous encounters prior to endeavoring a clean and clear path of success and self-realization.

Thus far, among many of the insightful topics covered in previous chapters, we have discussed the essentials to creating the life we desire by defining our self-love, passion and purpose; we covered how our thoughts and beliefs are carried out in our lives by way of our conversations and actions; we've discussed the importance of being tuned in to our emotions and using our feelings to gage how far we are from our perspective truths; we reviewed the Four A's (acceptance, alignment, attraction and allowance); we addressed being mentally, spiritually, emotionally, financially and physically prepared to receive into our lives everything required for self-realization; and, we also covered self-sabotage. Yet, as incredibly insightful as those principles may be, I wanted to briefly touch upon the topic of self-mastery, and how it contributes to our ability to be "okay enough" with ourselves to begin the journey of transition and transcendence right where we stand. It's all in the choice and decision to do so, based on our ability to increase, as well as, master the following aspects of who we truly are from the inside out:

- Self-acceptance (already covered in the Four A's)
- Self-awareness
- Self-discipline
- Self-perception (image, concept and esteem)

The intention of introducing these concepts at this point is so that we can begin to cultivate a level of insight and understanding about what it will take for us not only to begin our journey right where we are, but to enable us to sustain it when times get tough and cumbersome.

As mentioned earlier, *self-acceptance* is less about cowering to defeat, surrendering to victimization or allowing circumstances to dictate our fate as it is about knowing who we are - right now. Being fully capable of accepting who we are in this moment **is not *just* about appreciating our good points; it has more to do with being honest about our less commendable traits without judgment, guilt, or a sense of inadequacy.** It is about acknowledging who we are and disclosing the truth about *everything* we have done thus far in our lives, regardless of the cost or amount of pain. It also entails the recognition of strengths and weaknesses that will either promote evolution or hinder us from changing and improving our lives. All of this helps with building the type of confidence we will need in order to make the powerful decision to embark upon a path toward creating, having, being and experiencing desired realities.

To become *self-aware* is to recognize certain aspects of ourselves that are limiting us from loving ourselves fully and maximizing our highest potential. It entails shedding light on the false beliefs or half-truths we have created as a result of past occurrences, as well as, allowed to minimize our contribution to the world as wives, sisters, mothers, daughter, friend, etc. The moment we are able to break free from limiting beliefs is the moment we will begin to heal ourselves mentally, physically, spiritually and emotionally. After all, the past has already been lived and is now canceled from our current reality – that is, unless we choose to hold on to it. It would behoove us to reframe the painful events that occurred in our past and observe them as merely speed bumps designed to slow us down enough to focus on what really matters, rather than to compel us to quit. Even while driving, speed bumps are intended to slow our movement, make us cautious of our surroundings, protect others and ourselves from injury, and focus our attention to the road ahead. Metaphorically speaking, the speed bumps we encounter as challenges in our lives prepare us for that "something" soon to cross, or appear, that we may have missed had we continued speeding past. Rather than focusing on the discomfort of our "speed bumps" we can recognize that in spite of the bumps, scrapes and bruises we accumulated as a result of being unprepared, we managed to endure the road. How do we know this? We are still here. Being grateful for the blessing of a life remained, the "speed bumps" and the lessons helps with changing the trajectory of our quest for preferred states of existence. Now, in this moment, we owe it to ourselves to find the motivation required to press forward and toward the prize of our achievement and the fulfillment of our most desired experiences.

Personal management through *self-discipline* is a one of the special qualities we should invest the time in developing as it guarantees greater success, accomplishment and happiness in our lives. The cultivation of good habits and practices must become a way of life if we are to achieve anything worthwhile and lasting. Loving ourselves into our highest potential means embracing our worth, as well as the will to engage in long hours, weeks, months, or maybe even years of concentrated, disciplined work in a particular field, industry or platform. Success and genius don't always come by way of sheer talent or skill alone. It most often comes through our commitment to study, exert discipline, and tap into the grit that is required to exceed limitations. In order for us to become who we desire to be, we must be able to control impulses, emotions, desires and behaviors, especially those that can easily distract us from our path. The ability to resist immediate pleasure and instant gratification in favor of long-term focus must become a daily practice if we are ever to realize our greatest visions and aspirations.

And lastly, there is our *self-perception*. One thing working in our favor is that our self-perceptions can change. The intention is to be as accurate as we possibly can with how we see ourselves in the world and in relationship to others around us. Many of us fail to understand that how we experience the world and what we experience in our lives is directly related to how we think and feel about ourselves. We have to be careful not to over-inflate our self-image and conceive of things about ourselves that are inauthentic. A false sense of self-awareness is extremely dangerous in respect to attempting to create the life we desire. Conversely, this also applies to the opposite perspective where we become prone to allowing negatives self-images, weaknesses, and flaws to be exaggerated, or more pronounced in our thinking, believing, speaking and behaving. When our self-perception is skewed, we **limit our ability to access to the attitudes, beliefs, traits, qualities and characteristics that are required to help with transition** and transcendence in our lives. Thus, we should make it a daily practice to discover more about who we really are so that our outlook of possibility and potential is constantly growing.

The path to success and the fulfillment of our greatest dreams and aspirations begins with our willingness to cultivate characteristics and aspects of ourselves that promote fruition, so that we are constantly in alignment with what we desire to have, be and experience. We also need to take self-inventory of how we are being perceived, how we are communicating, and how we affect our environments, relationships and circumstances. The more we are able to grow more aware, accept, and then love ourselves just as we are, right where we are, the more capable we will be to tap into the passion behind our goals and ultimately the purpose for our lives. Why? Because through this effort recognizing the value and meaning of our lives gets easier. Because we became less interested in creating excuses and justifications and more invested in seeking opportunities to share love, exactly as we are without apology.

Rising from Within

Resisting the wrongs, injustices, and acts of cruelty in society is the price we pay for the gift of life with which we have been so greatly blessed.
— Dr. James Lawson

Here's what I believe: if we, as human beings, were to let go of all the things that are trivial or irrelevant to the truth of who we *really* are on the inside; if we were to focus on the aspects of ourselves that uniquely distinguish us from the rest of humanity; if everyone in the world took the time to cultivate their spirituality in order to be more loving, compassionate, or of selfless service to everyone around them, then the world would be a much happier place to live. Think about it: if we were all to commit to be the highest version of ourselves, to flourish beyond physical, spiritual, emotional, and financial limitations, the course of the planet would be altered to one that is more conducive to spreading love, kindness, and compassion. There'd be a significant decrease in the pain and misery that seems so rampant today.

Based on conversations I have had with several people over the past couple of years, as well as what is being conveyed in mainstream media, there seems to be a collective sense that the world is out of alignment with the true intention of our existence: to seek wisdom, discover our purpose, pursue deeper levels of happiness, and share love unconditionally. This is also evidenced by the increase in protests against patriarchal oppression and racially motivated acts of violence throughout the country – or even around the world. Clearly, we have reached what feels to be the highest state of hate this country has ever seen. We have collectively replaced feelings of hope with the sentiments of hurt. Fear of harm and disregard has replaced what used to be our enthusiasm for life. We are feeling the pain that is directly resultant of social disparity in income and education. The contagious urge for immediate gratification, as well as the accumulation of wealth, contributes greatly to our collective inclination to be distracted by frivolous attainment, rather than staying focused on what matters most.

Because of this, I would like to take a moment to encourage each of us to somehow find a way to utilize our disappointments in ways that are constructive and lean more toward the healing we all hope for. Let us use our disapproval of racial, gender, sexual, or cultural oppression and virulence as motivation to actively participate in the prevention of societal collapse; if not for ourselves, then let us do it for the next generations.

Whenever I get hopeless, or even sensitive to the acts of oppression, injustice, and inequality of the world, I like to recall the words of four outstanding leaders, who contributed greatly to the forward movement of humanity in America: Leo Tolstoy, Mother Teresa, Dr. Martin Luther King, Jr., and Rumi.

> *Everyone thinks of changing the world, but no one thinks of changing himself.* - Leo Tolstoy
>
> *I alone cannot change the world, but I can cast a stone across the waters to create many ripples.* - Mother Teresa
>
> *Injustice anywhere is a threat to justice everywhere.* - Martin Luther King, Jr.
>
> "Yesterday I was clever, so I wanted to change the world. Today I am wise, so I am changing myself." – Rumi

It's true, these legendary leaders (human rights activists in their own right) may not have stood specifically for the rights and equal treatment of women per se, yet they stood for the freedom and liberation for *everyone*. Yet, in recognizing that none of us are here in this life to win the Olympics of oppression, they offered inspiration that compels the compassionate people of this world to stand for *anyone* who is oppressed (irrespective of the culture, class, gender group to which one belongs), or a victim of subjugation and inequity, including you. Because of this, we as women must understand that the greatest expression of activism, or the resistance of oppression, is to own, and then stand in our power, our love, and our innate ability to create. Better yet, the greatest gift we could ever offer children in upcoming generations is to fully realize our potential exactly how we envision in our dreams and aspirations. We must harness the thoughts, beliefs, and emotions stirring inside our hearts to rise above areas in our respective lives where we are *internally* oppressed. The moment we begin to see ourselves as the source of light, love, hope, and inspiration to the people around us, taking on the responsibility of personal fulfillment gets easier. Fulfillment is crucial to not only our survival, but it is also vital to positively altering the course of the world's evolution.

Not only do I recognize the undying will to thrive (not just survive) in spite of conditions and circumstances playing out in my own life, but I also see it in the countless lives of women I have met throughout my years of coaching and training. The truth of the matter is that 95% of the people I meet wish they were doing something other than what they are doing. I would say that most people I meet are not doing what they love in life. Many are sacrificing their happiness for the sake of survival – paying bills, feeding children, taking care of parents, etc. Some don't know how to reach for their dreams. Plenty are too overwhelmed at the thought of fruition that they are overtly petrified and incapable of taking the first step. Some don't know where to even begin. Others can't afford it. Many are too afraid of failure, or even success. Most feel that the act of casting the concerns of taking risks to the wind is too hard, and the costs of being an outcast is too high. Many of us make the easy choice to live safely within the solid white lines of conformity. Needless to say, I am often amazed at how many of us have developed the habit of suppressing the things we really want, or want to be in life, for the sake of comfort.

Life is complicated. Wouldn't you agree? Don't get me wrong, this is not to say that I believe we are all doomed to a life of misery and strife. In fact, I am attempting to convey to you what is possible when we accept things as they are, while at the same time, strive to focus on the possibilities that exist on the brighter side of our lives. I am saying that, rather than blindly fighting against the world *as it is*, we must begin to acquiesce to the truth that the world around us is filled with problems that can seem overly complex at times; problems that have us feeling discouraged and disappointed when we dwell on them too long. As shared in previous chapters, acceptance is the first step to creating the changes we wish to see – in our lives, and in the world. As daunting as "fixing the world" can seem (clearly, there isn't a *single* person who could "fix" the ills of an entire society on their own), I would bet my life that there are more people in this world who desire to help solve the world's issues than not. As both writer and reader of this book, I am prompted to believe that we share the aspiration to contribute to change and healing. At the very least, we are ready to lift our heads from beneath the sand and make some sort of effort to make a difference in this society, even if only through our individual lives, or the lives of our children. We have united at this crossroads of *staying the same* or r*ising above helplessne*ss for a reason. Thus, we must lean on one another, and inspire each other to begin harnessing the dormant talents and gifts within so that we can be *the change we wish to see in the world.*

If you are like me, someone who is in constant contemplation on how to make a significant difference in the world, then I am certain you encounter days where the thought of achieving such a task seems utterly impossible. However, here is a *huge* lesson I have learned in recent weeks: changing my world *is* changing the world. Remember this: changing our world begins with our ability to see everything, and everyone (including ourselves), through the lens of love. It also entails filtering every thought, belief, perspective, and action through love. Love is the key to changing not only *our personal worlds*, but also the world that is constantly evolving around us. In fact, the influx of compassion, love, happiness, and healing most of us hope to see in the world, starts with our individual determination to discover those very things inside ourselves. The wiser we grow, the easier it is to recognize how the notion that true happiness can be cultivated through the attainment of material wealth and external validation, makes absolutely no sense. The *things* we obtain along our respective journeys have nothing at all to do with love, nor do they contribute toward our need to heal, or correct, the aspects of our lives that hinder us from sustaining happiness.

Through all my trials, I have discovered that the journey to happiness is actually much shorter than any journey I could ever traverse across a proverbial rainbow. For me, the journey began with finding the courage to make one single choice: *to love myself in ways that grants me the freedom to live fully expressed, and without apology*. The best decision I've made in my life, thus far, is centered on my willingness to live my life *as I see fit*, rather than what others see fit for me. Trust me, it isn't always an easy commitment to uphold. Yet, I believe I am able to make this choice daily by continuously working to reshape my beliefs, increase myself worth, and liberate myself from previous conditionings that once restricted me from listening and dancing to the beat of my own drum. I know that if I ever were to make a different choice, I could never fully recover the parts of myself that are still buried beneath the negative beliefs about my potential that have been passed down from my parents, their parents, and their parents before them, etc.

The other day, while in conversation with my mentor, I was subtly reminded of something that has been essential to my growth and evolution as a woman: *there is not one person, situation, or relationship; no condition, pattern or behavior learned in my rearing, that can stop me from reaching my destiny*. The only person who can keep me from realizing my destiny is ME. Of course, there are those limiting conditions that I have subconsciously picked up consequent to my past experiences. However, the choice to allow them to *remain* the reasons I fall short of reaching full potential is no one else's doing but my own. Thus, the will to rise above excuses and limitations will always prompt me to own my truths, as well as love myself more than the need to hold on to any of those inherited beliefs. This was, and continues to be, yet another challenging practice I am committed to maintaining. I am not alone in this struggle. I know because, today, there are millions of women like me, who have been conditioned (by parents, peers, significant others, or society at large) to love everyone else on the planet *first and* love themselves last.

I'd like to offer a bit of insight that I hope will help you rid your mind of beliefs which imply that it is not only selfish to love yourself *first,* but also that you are not worthy of loving everything about who you are, as well as who you are not. Loving yourself starts with becoming attuned with *what you need.* Next, tell the truth about certain aspects of yourself that have been suppressed and unlived for much longer than you prefer. Then, tell the truth about why it is you have allowed these aspects of yourself to lie dormant for so long. All of this will entail having some tough conversations with yourself. Hearing the answers to the inquiries will require that you place yourself in the center of this moment, not in the past where you were hurt and conditioned to believe you are "less-than," and not in the future where you fear encountering more of what you've already experienced in your past. Find whatever courage you can muster to begin granting permission to elevate your self-worth; to override all the negative thoughts and opinions that others may have shared about you.

Overcoming Internal Suppression Resultant of Our Buts

Experience provides us our greatest lessons, and these lessons enable us to master the things that prohibit the right to choose for ourselves in ways that are loving and liberating. The more lessons we accrue, the wiser we become. Hindsight will eventually reveal how our whole lives have been shaped around the social pressure to conform to behaviors, beliefs, and attitudes that society and culture deem normal. Our successes and failures have always been measured by our willingness to subscribe to these inherited set of norms. From an early age, we learn of the rewards that come as a result of minding our parents, suppressing our thoughts and emotions, completing our education, getting a job, finding a spouse, buying a house with a two-car garage, having 2.5 children, and then, training our children to follow the same path that was laid for us. Repercussions of failing to abide by these conditions often result in shame, rejection, judgement, or abandonment. And, because we will do everything in our power to avoid feelings of being judged as abnormal, we comply. Absently, we pass the criteria to fit in with the Status Quo of performing, and behaving, on to the next generation, failing to understand that the ways of society has nothing at all to do with who we *really are, or who your children will become*. If we were to step back and take a good look at what we are choosing, we would find that attempting to fit into these societal norms is the most oppressive choice we could make on our own behalf.

Despite the level of ease that comes with choosing comfort over freedom and truth, it still is a choice that is harmful to our growth and potential as a human being. Most of us fail to recognize all that is forfeited (blessings, opportunities to be a blessing, prosperity, loving relationships, wisdom, etc.) when we neglect to carve out a life path that fits more with who we are on the inside. Deep inside, we know that to follow the norm is to take the road most traveled when it comes to "making something out of our lives." Yet, and still, everyone who chooses to conform is unhappy and unfulfilled in their lives, in one way or another. What do you think would come of our lives if we often reminded each other that we are all merely a thought away from being exactly what we have been uniquely designed to be? The moment we decide to begin living our lives as they have been uniquely and divinely designed, we become greater contributors to the world at large. We become human rights activists in our own right.

Activism through Self-Fulfillment

There are so many people in this world who have been born with the vigor to make a difference in this world through protests, marching, campaigning, and resisting systems and establishments that limit the life and potential of people. I have come into the awareness that not everyone is made to resist inequality and injustice in this capacity. Yet, this does not negate the fact that each of us is charged with the responsibility of leaving this world better than when we arrived. Whether we choose to adhere to this responsibility or not is a personal decision. What I realize today is that our individual contribution to the collective desire for justice, equality, and healing through the use of our gifts and talents to make money to give to causes, is just as effective as any other demonstration of resistance to wrong doing. Another thing I realize is that it is impossible for any of us to give what we do not have. Hence the reason it is imperative that each one of us walk the focused and narrow path of doing everything we can to become exactly what we envision. This choice alone will set us on the path to seeing, meeting, and acquiring whatever is needed for us to live in fullness, and as the highest expression of who we are innately. We owe it to each other. We owe it to our babies. We owe it to the world.

There is a reason why fulfillment and service are our highest ambition in life, which is exactly why I am always encouraging the people I meet to ask themselves one vital question: *Am I doing {insert action here} because I want to, or am I doing {insert action here} because society says I should?* You see, another reason why many of us are so disgruntled with our lives is because there seems to be insufficient opportunities to give of ourselves fully through our gifts, talents, and passions, and still make a decent living, or enough to provide for our families. The inability to see alternative possibilities existing beyond our current reality, which is already in in complete contrast to what we silently prefer, makes rising above excuses and limitations feel insurmountable. We believe the undesired and unappealing aspects of our life experiences are simply "the hands we are dealt." But if we were to make a small shift in perspective, we could begin to perceive limitation, or restriction, as opportunities to make different choices that are more in alignment with who we were divinely designed to be. The thought that we are only entitled to settling for the aspects of our lives that we do not desire or prefer is fear based and driven by the ego's need to keep you in the cycle of failure and incompletion. Rather, they are opportunities to liberate ourselves, to deconstruct limiting beliefs about what we conceive about what is possible.

To me, the debate about whether or not there is a significant decline in morality, not to mention equality, in today's society is indisputable. Some of us would even argue that the shift in morality should not be perceived as a decline, but rather a change in times meant to usher us into the next evolution of possibility and potential as humans. The fear of the unfamiliar, the unknown, and the unpredictability of our future has become evident in the way we behave toward one another. Our inclination to bemoan the current state of the world, as well as the tragedies and atrocities we witness on a daily basis, may be resultant of our insistence on clamoring for the days passed. What we do not realize is that it is impossible to create anything new in our lives when we keep our eyes pointed at the rearview mirror. If we were to shift our gaze to the mirror standing before us, we will see reflecting back to us one amazing reality: it is only in the current moment that we can reach any level of fulfillment that could potentially contribute toward the changes we wish to see in the world. Despising today, and holding on to the past, sets the stage for us to relive fear and pain, over and over again.

Recognizing the impermanent nature of reality helps us to remember that *nothing* stays the same. When standing in the light of "everything changes," we attain clarity around the fact that all things are possible. If nothing stays the same, then the opportunity to change our circumstances always lies before us. The trick is in endeavoring the following:
- Refrain from blindly and impulsively reacting to things you do not prefer – about yourself, your life circumstances, and your relationships.
- Detach yourself from negative thoughts as often as possible.

This gets easier once you are able to understand that you are not your thoughts; thoughts are forms of energy that can be selected, dismissed, transformed, or created.
- Discern what is true about who you are. Then, learn to make choices that are more in alignment with your deepest truths, needs, and desires.
- Reconnect with the deepest aspects of who you are that have remained unlived for far too long.

The most vital lesson I have learned thus far is that my desire to be the change I wish to see in the world (through legacy and activism) can never be fully implemented if I am not first fulfilled in my own life. As long as I am unfulfilled, I remain incapable of providing myself love. As long as I am incapable of providing myself love, I remain incapable of offering myself to the world as a loving, purpose-driven individual. I mention this because we as women have been groomed to believe that the pursuit of self-love and fulfillment is a selfish act. My ask is that we consider the possibilities that would arise if we chose to recondition ourselves into believing in fulfillment and love as a form of activism, or a healthy form of protest against the pains and injustices of the world. What if we began to view our ambition for greatness, or at least the willingness to live our best selves as a way of contributing to the restoration of morality in this society? Imagine if we were to remove the stigma of selfishness from the choice to love ourselves first. I'd imagine the release of worry and concern would free us up to create exactly what we desire on the inside. In fact, I'd bet my life that we'd be uplifted, excited, and enthusiastic enough to move beyond obstacles and previously percieved limitations. All the more reason that we must cultivate courage, positive energy, and faith in the unseen, and the unknown, in order to confidently pursue our path to fulfillment.

Something else I've realized in recent months: many of the acts of oppression and subjugation occuring in the world around us is merely a reflection of what we may be suppressing the greatest parts of ourselves due to social conditioning. To be afraid, angry, or concerned about the state of the world part of the human experience. As women, we tend to be a little bit more emotionally sensitive to many of the abhorrent tragedies occurring. In fact, the grief we experience in reaction to the worldy affairs is what makes it hard to turn our back and ignore the pain we are suffering as a collective. It is the compassion we hold for others that compels us *to do something*. That being the case, it is wise to remain mindful enough to view our sadness as a call to action. Know that it is our response to the underlying call within our sadness that will determine how far we go in our lives, especially in respect to our dreams and aspirations. Remember, the fruition of our dreams and aspirations contributes greatly to healing the world. Every product provided, or service rendered, as a result of following our dreams in some way supports the needs of another person.

Just as much as we can remain weighed down by sadness, we can just as well choose to use it to propel us to take action in spite our fears of not reaching our goals, not being enough, not being *good* enough, or any other "not" fears preventing us from taking the next best step toward healing. As long as we cower to our fears, we will never be able to confront the things designed to help us to rise to the "next level" in our lives. Here is a dose of reality I would like to bring to our collective awareness: *whether we like it or not, the truth is that the entertainment of our buts and excuses is a form of internal oppression.* This idea gets easier to digest when we consider who and how we are failing to show up in the world, or more intimately, how we are neglecting in the lives of those closest to us, when we opt not to follow our dreams and aspirations. We could even contemplate how our absence will continue to negatively impact the lives and communities that need what we have to offer to realize their own greatness. So, from this perspective, we owe the world our liberation from habitual *butting*, or using excuses as reasons to play it safe in life. The willingness to overcome our excuses and make steps toward our destinies makes us activists in our own right.

My Personal Liberation

Adding this chapter in the revised edition of Let Go of Your But! is resultant of an epiphany I had that derives from the Universal law titled, *So within, So without.* (The law basically simplifies what I have mentioned earlier about our outer world reflecting our inner world; our outer world and the things created, or tolerated, in our reality mirrors what we believe to be true on the inside of us). My epiphany: *see without, go within.* I have come to recognize the opportunity to see what I am lacking (seeing *without*) in the world around me and using it as a reflection of what may be absent inside of me (go *within*).

Such an earth-shattering awakening served as the underlying reason I made the conscious decision to change my birth name, Kimberly E. Banks, to Naje Aditi Badu (which means, "queen who is powerful beyond measure, strong, and *free*"). Giving myself a name that is more in alignment to who I am truly, was a way for me to begin altering my experience of the *world from the inside out*. It has been one of the biggest steps I've taken toward healing and harnessing the divine power within for me to create exactly what I have been sent here to create. For years, I have studied countless books, spiritual principles, teachings, and philosophies, yet none of those scripts equipped me with the sense of freedom for which I'd sought for most of my adult life.

Seeing what I was lacking (*without*), and then taking the journey *within*, enabled me to recognize that I had (and still have) challenges with rising above certain conditions and beliefs. More specifically, I struggled with releasing conditions and beliefs that no longer serve me; that no longer support me in my quest to realize my destiny. I was able to recognize the need to release such limiting thoughts and ideas about who or what I thought I was supposed to be as a woman. Rather than continuing to suppress the most vivid aspects of who I really am, I granted myself permission to become who I am meant to be. I allowed the real me, Naje Badu, to emerge exactly as God intended. Consequently, I am gaining momentum, and embracing the courage to be *alright* with allowing the monk and the activist, both aspects of me that have been lying dormant since birth, the freedom to exist without restriction or hindrance.

Just as I have granted myself permission to simply *begin the journey* of making a true contribution toward liberation - both internally and in the world, I hope to inspire you to do the same. Why now, you may be asking? Well, you'd have to be living under a rock not to notice the influx of women around the world rising up against self-imposed or societal limitations and conditioning, especially in America. Our collective willingness to embrace the courage to say "enough is enough" has to be the greatest illustration of "letting go of your but" I have witnessed in my lifetime. The beautiful display of empowerment should hold us all accountable to, not just the women of this era who are tying up their bootstraps and trudging through the mud of intersectional inequality, but also for the women who paved the way for our current social liberties in the past. Also, we must hold ourselves accountable to the next generation of women who will rise tomorrow as a result of our choice to lead by example.

The Impact of Seeing Without
   "It is very difficult to go through life when your core belief about yourself is that you are incompetent and do not count. When you have no sense of your own value, you are like a leaf in the wind, dependent on what others think of you to know who you are." — *Valerie Porr*

In recent months, I have managed to allow a small, yet significant shift in perspective of life to alter how I experience the circumstances and situations that arise daily: change doesn't come *to me;* it comes *from me. Conflicts that arise in my relationships, circumstances, and situations are designed to help me focus my attention inward to discover where it is my spirit requires modification in another area of my life.* Every single day of our lives the opportunity to either yield to the way things are or stand firmly in the decision to change them. Just know that giving in to ease and comfort or choosing not to change your circumstances is a form of self-loathing.

Here is also where I offer a bit of tough love. Let's go back to the term I referenced a moment ago: *self-loathing.* Such an unpleasant concept, wouldn't you agree. It's so extreme, so harsh. The idea of loathing anything brings about such a negative connotation, especially when the thing being loathed is your*self.* Yet, and still, the habit of unconscious self-loathing has certainly become the plague that sits at the epicenter of individual and societal suffering. With all of the stresses we encounter in life, it's easy to surmise how we have lost connection with who we truly are as individuals, as women, and as human beings. Based on the atrocities we are seeing in the world, the need for emotional restitution is evident. The average person remains vastly underinformed about who they are, let alone the history of how they came to be. There are a litany of pathologies, thoughts, beliefs, and habits many of us have inherited, and then carried out. It is the maintenances of such ideas that led us to this very moment in our lives. The worst part about it is that most of our self-loathing beliefs have been suppressed well beneath the subconscious, which makes it very difficult to be aware of how our negative self-perceptions impact our daily lives. This is not to minimize any of our previous struggles, sacrifices, and successes that got us this far, but it is time that we begin to consider how we wish to write the next chapter of our book.

If I may, I'd like to share with you a few words of inspiration expressed by the esteemed social justice activist, Tamika Mallory (Co-

Founder of the Women's March organization). In a recent speech she said, "any issue that plagues our larger community, plagues our personal community." This statement is a more reserved cousin to the statement I shared earlier, *"see without, go within."* Though she may have been speaking of the tragedies and perils we are currently encountering in the world, I'd like to shed light on an opportunity to delve one more layer deeper to include our "self" in this piece of enlightenment. Doing this will help us to maintain accountability for all of the actions, thoughts (conscious and subconscious), and beliefs that ultimately impact our world (larger community), our cultural and social tribes (our personal community), and lastly, ourselves. Reminder: no matter how much we desire to stand for justice and freedom in the world, it is impossible to achieve this without first standing for, and then exercising, freedom in our own lives. An easy place for us to begin the process of personal liberation is to become more mindful of the conversations we maintain in our minds about who we are, what we deserve, and what is possible. There is a quote that reads, "If someone talked to you the same way you talk to yourself, you would have kicked them out of your life a long time ago." Recognize that the way we view ourselves is reflected in the way others treat us. This statement is applicable toward both the good and the not so pleasant experiences we encounter in life.

Overcoming Unworthiness

Unworthiness is another sentiment that impacts our experience of life and the world at large. I recently attended a meditation and sound healing class and was gifted with an unforeseen spiritual reading. I remember feeling simultaneous emotions of freedom and sadness while she was speaking. She offered me this insight: *You are relevant. You are loved. Even though people may not tell you as often as you'd like. You may not receive all of the accolades and admiration that may be owed to you at times, but you are very relevant. The world needs you. You mean so much to the world, and you are making an impact, even when you can't see it. You have to continue speaking your truth. You have a voice that is relevant. Use it. Don't be afraid.*

I walked out of the meditation session aware that I must have been carrying some sentiments that were in contrast with her revelation. I cried at the thought that somewhere in my subconscious I must have been feeling unloved, unfulfilled and disregarded. Of course, as an empath, the woman shared several uplifting messages to confirm I am on the right path in my life. However, the reason I mention the part of being reminded about my relevance in this world is we have a tendency to forget who we are and what we are meant to bring into this life. I wanted to remind you of the alternative to harboring low self-esteem, despair, and the consistent need to maintain negative perspectives. These are also symptoms of our self-hatred. Sometimes we are oblivious to the fact that we maintain a victim mentality, instead of rising above the lies and excuses we tell ourselves about what's possible in our lives. Not to mention our inclination to judge, criticize, and offer defeating opinions about other people, and surrounding circumstances. The proclivity to focus more on the suffering in life is resultant of being weighed down by the pain of being unfulfilled and feeling unworthy of what we truly desire. This, My Friend, is always, and will always be a form of self-loathing.

Many of us suffer from the self-loathing dynamic as we live in a society that places significant emphasis on perfection and achievement. No matter how successful one may be or how much money he or she makes in their respective life, loss in competition can leads to self-doubt. Why? Because most of us are endeavoring a never-ending quest for recognition and validation from external sources. We have been conditioned to constantly evolve in to something or someone other than who, or what, we are innately. What we are missing, however, is the underlying need to avoid the pain of being disappointed with who we are in the current moment.

Self-Compassion

Now, more than ever, the change we wish to see in the world must begin with our choice to be compassionate with ourselves, and then extending that compassion to others who harbor pain, as well. If you are having a difficult time knowing where to begin administering self-compassion, you can start by cultivating a healthy attitude though the following practices:

- *Self-Kindness:* Practice replacing harsh criticism and judgement about yourself with kindness, patience, and understanding.
- *Common Humanity:* Eliminate the practice of separation and alienation; respect the commonality of suffering that exists inside everyone. Allow yourself to remain open to being a light, or source of healing for everyone you encounter.
- *Mindfulness*: Recognize the pain of your life experience is not an isolated incident. Use this awareness to alter any thoughts and beliefs you maintain about another person or group. Minimize your inclination to gossip, pass judgement, or maintain thoughts of ill-will against others.
- *Love Unconditional:* Extend love without condition. Open your heart and be mindful of the energy you espouse or extend in any given moment. Filter every thought, perspective and belief through the lens of love.
- *Forgiveness:* Release the pain and negative attitudes toward those who have hurt you. Remember, holding on to past pain only hurts you, rather than the person who hurt you.
- *Bold and Unapologetic Truth Sharing:* No matter how much it hurts, tell the truth to and about yourself or your life, to and about others, to and about the circumstances that occur in our collective lives.

Being a person who shares the truth, no matter what, is not

easy.

Often, the truth we know is the truth we avoid; or the truth we need to share with others is the truth we suppress. However, the more we suppress the truth, the less chances we have at liberating ourselves from fears, limitations, and societal conditions that keep us from bringing to fruition our greatest desires.

Case in point: for years I kept this book on the shelf, letting it gather dust while I avoided the feelings of failure of not bringing to fruition the vision I had for this project. Yet, I had to realize, that I was the only one who stopped me from carrying out my vision. No one else was responsible. So, the truth I will share with you is that this fourth edition of the book has been penned because I was able to finally accept the fact that *I dropped the ball*. I gave up on my vision because getting speaking gigs was much harder than I thought; because not as many people bought the book as I envisioned; because the notoriety I'd hoped to gain as an author evaded me. Who knows where I would be now had I not gone through a major depression; a dark experience that was resultant of me giving up on my original dream a couple of years prior. All I know is that, as I am sitting down to rewrite this edition, the opportunity to realize my dream still exists before me. However, the only way I could move forward with stepping into my full potential is for me to tell the truth about not only my shortcoming, but also about the self-loathing I had been maintaining about my own inability to overcome negative thoughts and excuses (go figure, as an author of a book of this nature). Also, I had to tell the truth about how many people beyond myself I'd failed on account of not carrying out the intention God placed in my heart, which ultimately meant that I failed the people who would benefit from the fruit of such labor.

Naturally, carrying the weight of all insecurity, shame, hopelessness, and disappointment became too much to suppress. Deep down I knew I had to find a way to release all of the negative energy that typically comes with failure; otherwise, the desire to progress in any other area of my life would continue to evade me. Eventually, I stood before a mirror, with tears streaming down my face, until I found the courage to tell the woman staring back at me, a simple truth:

It is your divine right to love yourself fully and completely. It is your divine responsibility to do everything in your power to become what God designed you to be. It is your divine duty to be the best version of yourself so that others can learn how to love themselves enough to reach their own destiny. It is your divine assignment to be a beacon of light and hope for others who are afraid of failing. You must rise. You must thrive. You must lean into hope and faith, until you move through the fear and the pain, and create a new reality for yourself. Have hope. Love yourself. Stay the course.

If you are weighed down by negative thoughts about your failures and shortcomings, I encourage you to have the same type of conversation with yourself. It is both powerful and liberating, to say the least. Tears may fall, but with them come the release of shame, guilt, and regret. Let them fall and allow yourself to be cleansed. Be an activist; one who recognizes that your voice and your purpose are powerful beyond the limitations and excuses that have hindered you thus far. Fight for the life you desire to live. Fight for your life so that others are inspired to do the same with their own. Do everything in your power to be everything you envision. Replace your fears with hope, so that you can be clear in your mind, body, heart, and spirit as you take the next best step toward liberation and healing. In the meantime, I leave you with the words of Senator Corey Book, who says, "Hope isn't some kind of Polly-Annish thing that says, 'things are going to get better.' No! Hope is seeing the ugliness, the wretchedness, the darkness of the reality in which we live and having the conviction that despair will never have the last word."

Taking Time

"You may not control all the events that happen to you, but you can decide not to be reduced by them."

- Dr. Maya Angelou

My editor asked me why I opted to make this chapter the last in this book, rather than placing what I am about to share at the beginning, where it could potentially have a monumental impact and substantiate my reasoning for writing this book. Remember, I declared in the earlier part of this book that we are on this journey of evolution together. After further deliberation, I have concluded that the sharing of this story at the close of this volume would have a much greater impact being that we will be segueing into the topic of "self-mastery" in the next book of this series. Being that I am taking the layered approach in delivering this series, making the hand off between self-love and the need for self-mastery will most certainly enable us to continue the course of evolving, improving, making healthier choices and decisions, as well as maintaining alignment with the life we truly desire. One of the intentions I set out to fulfill through the *Let Go of Your But!* project is to create a sense of community and support for us as women as we endeavor to reach our highest dreams and aspirations. The decision to remain utterly unveiled and honest with readers was made to ensure my commitment to the sisterhood. Peeling back layers and being vulnerable with an audience is not a strong suit possessed by many authors who comprise inspirational or motivational content. The inclination is usually towards sharing the insight obtained through trial and tribulation yet neglecting to expose the actual moments of adversity that gave birth to lessons learned. We opt to hide behind the mistakes, the challenges, the poor choices or even the backsliding perpetuated by the lack of courage and willpower for the sake of maintaining our pristine image of *teacher* or expert.

Needless to say, it is seldom easy to place ourselves in the position to be scrutinized, judged, rejected, labeled, or misunderstood. However, I am choosing to take a different path in this moment, one that I hope will help you, the reader, to understand that, though I love my life and am appreciative of everything I have encountered throughout, I am not able to say I am where I aspire to be just yet. Having written this book, I am by no means attempting to appear flawless or exempt from making mistakes that greatly impact my life. This path I am on entails a commitment to strive for greatness and to always be better than I was a moment prior - no matter what level of success I achieve or the degree of the mistakes I make. Rather than concluding this book with the perception that I have "made it" or that I have tapped into a well of insight and wisdom that will make my life easy from here on out, I wanted to leave you with a clear understanding that a journey of self-love, self-mastery and self-actualization is constant and never-ending. Thus, what I am electing to do is reveal what it truly means to remain faithful to purpose, passion, and meaning that resides deep in our hearts, even despite contrasting surroundings resultant of the choices, decisions and mistakes made along the way.

I have invested a great amount of time researching and reflecting specifically on what appears to be the woman's challenge of successfully and effectively allocating efforts, enthusiasm, and energy across various areas of her life, and still maintain her power to wholeheartedly manifest her deepest desires. I am fully aware that this perception may not be applicable to every woman reading or listening to this book. However, I have come across enough women who share the same challenge and can relate to just how deterring this limitation can be in our lives. I am one of several women I know who would love to master aspects of themselves and achieve our greatest aspirations much like we seem to successfully master the roles we play in our families, relationships, friendships, and sometimes even our careers. So many women with whom I have spoken share the struggle of understanding how to outwardly express and live as the woman who dwells at the core of her being - the woman who remains stifled as a result of doing what she thinks is expected of her, rather than being true and authentic to her desires. Having discovered that I was not alone in the battle of balancing life aspirations with responsibilities, I wanted to broach the subject so that we may clearly identify and remedy potential areas of disparity in our lives. The idea is to demonstrate what it may take for us to decide *today* to show up in life, exactly as we envision, without apology, without fear of being judged and criticized for being audacious enough to choose self-*fullness*.

As I share with you the struggle of attaining achievement in my life, I am not just speaking about what it took to attain a job I really love, host my first solo art exhibit in fifteen years, follow my passion of writing, complete this book, or even become a Division II College Women's basketball official – all of which are monumental in the evolution of my life. I am talking about the decision to create a desired life by doing the work it takes to overcome conflicting mindsets. The decision to pursue self-love, increase self-awareness, embrace self-mastery, and practice self-acceptance in order to reach self-actualization is one that created the biggest shift of my life. To give you a better understanding of what I mean, travel with me down memory lane to a period in my life when prior visions of success were ultimately eclipsed by the ever-growing mountain of perceived failures I'd accumulated in my mind. As you will see, it is only when this perspective had begun to get the better part of me that I was able to make a shift and tap in to the self-love and worthiness required for me to pull myself out of the trenches.

For starters, let me disclose to you the mindset I'd maintained most of my life, while at the same time pursuing the essential "something greater for me" that maintained a relentless grip around my heart. It took a long time for me to recognize that, though I had endeavored to bring to reality various aspirations, my mindset and outlook for life was not in alignment with them. It wasn't until recently that I began to understand why the success I envisioned and strived for over the years, always managed to escape me. Looking back, I am able to really see how, without any true direction, purpose and focus, I'd squandered my talent and intelligence to lack and limitation. I can't say that I *truly* believed in my potential to reach success, to overcome unconscious self-sabotage to reach the end result of that whatever dream I was chasing. Not recognizing that each failed attempt left an annulling imprint in the very fibers of my internal beliefs. Negativity and discouragement kept me from seeing anything through to its completion. Whenever the ceiling of hindrance appeared, I gave up on my quest and looked to greener grasses, telling myself that success on that specific path "must not have been meant for me." Not once did it ever dawn on me to continue the course in spite how things appeared. I simply diverted my enthusiasm and attention to another endeavor, hoping to reach success through a venture that seemed less challenging. I did this repeatedly, praying to hit the jackpot. That is, until I began to recognize a pattern: with each unfinished venture I allowed to fall through the cracks, the more compelled I felt to start another, to somehow prove that the underlying belief of *success not being in the cards for me* could be overridden. The more enthusiastic about each new venture I became, the longer my list of unfinished projects grew. The longer my list of half-completed endeavors grew, the more I began to feel like a disappointment and a failure. The more discouraged I felt, the more insecure and uncertain I grew about my abilities to achieve *something,* or *anything* for that matter. Unbeknownst to me, the inner struggle of self-love and self-esteem eventually began to bleed into other aspects of my life, which ultimately affected how I showed up in the world, as well as my ability to believe in not only what was possible, but of what I considered myself worthy.

Eventually, my level of worthiness reached an all-time low. Poor choices resulted in a downhill spiral of unpleasant experiences within my relationships and financial circumstances. I allowed into my life some unfortunate situations as a result of feeling undeserving of having or being anything better. It wasn't until later that I was able to fully understand exactly why success and fulfillment seemed to evade me throughout those many years of stumbling and falling. Until then, happiness and success seemed utterly elusive.

It is a humbling experience to hit a wall and the only choice to make is to fall to your knees and surrender to struggle. There came a point in my life, not too long ago, where I realized that the older I'd grown over the years, the more experiences I accrued – some good, most substandard, a lot of them inferior. An awareness of how I'd gotten to this point was not evident until I was able to do some much-needed soul searching. In hindsight, I imagine it all occurred, not because I was a knucklehead (as my Dad used to say), but because I was never *certain* about what I was going to make of my life. To arrive at that awareness in the early forties, however, is just about crippling, especially since I'd placed great efforts toward studying, experimenting, and reaching for dreams that no one other than myself believed in - or so I thought. Even with all of my many efforts, and even though I knew what I wanted to *do*, and even though I could hear greatness calling my name, I had no idea how to face myself in its direction in order to reach fulfillment.

The impact of setting out to create greatness, while simultaneously holding negative beliefs, patterns, and mindsets that hinder growth and evolution, was both detrimental and beneficial. I know now that a conflict of desire and belief is not profitable. The strength and widened perspective I gained because of the lessons woven within each painful experience is priceless. Despite giving what I thought was my best effort to "love myself beyond self-sabotage and through to my highest potential," I continuously made the mistake of neglecting to alter my core beliefs about who I was, and what I was capable of having, being, and doing. Today, I know that beauty and love is borne of our ability to be naked, vulnerable, and unshielded of the need to protect us from judgment, criticism, and humiliation. Therefore, I am choosing to share the good, and the not so good, in my life. However, I ask that you pay close attention, to see if there are aspects in the story that are relatable to your own experience. Why? Because for the sake of learning from each other's mistakes, I am opting to disclose the devastation I encountered in the six-year span between the time I left corporate to venture out on my own as an entrepreneur and the moment I sat down to write this book (keep in mind, this doesn't include a plethora of challenges I experienced prior to this period, or even after).

The biggest hardship of my life started just one year after attempting to get a motivational speaking business off the ground, when it had become glaringly apparent that I was incapable of generating the income I'd envisioned. As with everything else before, the moment I ran out of money, and things got difficult, staying the course became extremely challenging. I immediately began looking for something else in which to prevail, and something else into which I could place my hope. Again, I failed to recognize that my commitment to succeed flew out the window the moment financial resources became scarce. With no income, I thought I had no other choice but to throw in the towel.

Naturally, I found myself in dire need of a job. Keep in mind, working for a boss, rather than being a boss, was something that, at the time, I was not at all eager to embrace. The irony is that I'd made a promise to myself to never return to the corporate world since I was utterly disgusted with the corporate politics, antics, and brown-nosing that was required for the sake of gaining well deserved recognition for my expertise and talent, not to mention a promotion. The truth was that I'd left the corporate environment to start my own business because I was exhausted with having to beg for someone to deem me worthy of increase in compensation and advancement. I was tired of having my talent and passion for leadership and greatness underutilized. I was tired of playing Russian Roulette, relying heavily upon the people who signed my paycheck every two weeks. Interestingly enough, consequent to poor preparation and planning, I had suddenly found myself headed back into the not-so-welcoming arms of corporate America. Due to a tainted outlook, my ego's resistance made my pursuit of employment extremely daunting and unbearable. Looking back, it's no wonder opportunities remained hidden from my view of possibility. I could not find a job to save my life - literally.

As if failure of my biggest try in life was not enough, it seemed as if everything that occurred after that only added to my pain and suffering. I lost my best friend to cancer. I was still during sadness and grief when an unexpected avalanche came piling down upon me. For the second time in my life (the first being in my late twenties), I was staring in the face of homelessness due to having to foreclose on a condo that I could no longer afford. Luckily, I was able to room at a friend's house, but eventually that became a touch and go situation because money was scarce. In the meantime, I made do by serving as an in-home caretaker to my then roommate who experienced an unanticipated flare of a previously dormant illness. As the effects of her illness grew worse, so did her depression. In the blink of an eye, I was inadvertently forced to assume the role of a surrogate mother, since she was incapacitated. I wasn't the least bit prepared for this situation. Yet, it was a blessing in disguise, because as hard as it was, I was able to offer love and support someone who was in the middle of a health crisis - something that I was fortunate enough not to have to endure.

I managed to do all of this while attending Inner Vision Institute of Spiritual Development, which called for me to travel back and forth to Silver Springs, Maryland, once a month. Luckily, I received food stamps once a month which is what I traded for rent and then feed myself as much as I could. I had scraped together the remainder of my 401k to fulfill a lifelong dream of not only meeting my spiritual mentor, Iyanla Vanzant, but also attending her prestigious institute. The program was scheduled to last two years, but the last few cents I had left to my name ran out at the end of year one, which meant I was unable to return for the second year. Yet again, another appearance of failure.

I diverted my promise of hope toward the grind of refereeing recreation, middle school basketball games - sometimes as many as ten games a day. This was grueling, but I figured it was best that I put my knowledge of the game to some use. After a few months, I tried to make up for my last failed attempt of completing the spiritual development program by filing for financial aid and enrolling in online classes. My new aspiration: to get a degree in Psychology. I was yet again heedless about having found one more momentary diversion from having lost mostly all hope and ambition to succeed. Lo and behold, after six months of maintaining straight A's in a field of study I'd grown to love so much, and just eight months shy of receiving a Bachelor's degree (a lifelong endeavor after starting and stopping on numerous occasions), I was kicked out of school due to some personal circumstances that disqualified me from continuing to receive financial assistance. Little did I know it was resultant of what I will share in the next paragraph. Since I was unable to resolve this matter in a timely manner, I was forced to fold my cards once again.

Moreover, I found myself facing jail time as a result of a

warrant out for my arrest. Unbeknownst to me, my license had been suspended for an unpaid carpooling ticket and an unpaid registration that I couldn't afford. I had my car repossessed out of my driveway at 3 o'clock in the morning because I could no longer make the payments. For two years, I was literally a paycheck away from being out in the streets. There were a countless number of days when I found myself sleeping in a car loaned to me by a friend, or on the couch of an apartment building conference room, because I had no place else to sleep whenever my roommate and I were at odds.

I was not accustomed to this type of lifestyle. I was not raised to be irresponsible (by no means should I have equated the ambition to start a business with recklessness; it's just that the outcomes I experienced during this period seemed to be only applicable to people who were flighty, unstable, or immature). I was raised to do everything in my power to position myself so that I would never have to rely on other people to take care of me. I was used to having a savings and being organized with my finances and being strategic with my choices and decisions.

Truthfully, I'd heard the whispered reminders that I was bigger than my hardships and "failures." They came frequently, as my soul tried desperately to ease my shame and discomfort. Yet, I ignored them. I ignored the truest, most talented aspects of me that had begun begging me to thrive despite my external conditions. Deep down, I knew the circumstances at the time were truly a reflection of the lack of preparation - nothing more – and should not have been taken so personally. I knew that my surrounding conditions weren't meant to dictate who I really was on the inside. Still, finding solace was extremely challenging because I had *nothing*, not even a "pot to piss in" (as my mother would say). There was nothing I had to offer anyone without involving them in my mess. Thus, when it came to companionship, I settled for less than I truly deserved – a series of one emotionally-abusive relationship after another. Naturally, the demise of each encounter merely added to my ever-growing pile of pain and regret. At the time, it only made sense that I began throwing pity parties and blaming my parents for not supporting me the way I needed, and when I needed them most (as a child and an adult). It was the only thing that made me feel better. I suppose somewhere deep inside I needed something to substantiate the inability to believe I was something more than the hardship I was enduring.

It goes without saying that my will to succeed finally made its exit. Having come to this realization while standing alone in the middle of a tiny room of a home that was not my own was cumbersome. Eventually, i found part-time job paying $8.50 per hour (now mind you this is in 2013 and I am 41 years of age) I couldn't begin to fathom how I was going to get my life together. I remember suffocating in the billows of inadequacy as the walls caved in around me. Any idea of how to escape the destruction of my crumbling world was slow to reveal itself to me. I was literally dumbstruck, lost in utter confusion, as I contemplated reasons why I'd suddenly glanced up and had nothing to show for the life I'd led thus far. No degree, no children, no family, no completed book projects, no relationship...*nothing*. Logically, this made no sense to me. After all, I'd spent years spinning my wheels *trying* to write the next best seller, *trying* to complete the next blockbuster screenplay, *trying* to start a motivational speaking business, *trying* to start a sports apparel line, trying to start a greeting card line. The list can go on with the amount of attempts I made to start something *but* neglected to finish. The ambition was there, but the mindset to surmount the discomfort of my shortcomings and blunders was nowhere to be found.

Remember the several thousand dollars I borrowed from my 401k that I used to enroll into the divinity institute? Well, even that decision eventually came back around to bite me in the rear. Consequent to my incapacity to pay back the money, plus interest, in the time agreed, I wound up losing a major tax fight with the IRS that left me in over $97,000 in debt. Once the devastation finally wore, and after months of having money confiscated from my account, often leaving me without a cent to my name, I finally learned that an extremely large amount of that debt was due to a mistake made by the IRS. However, this was not before I'd managed to scrape together $5,000 to hire a tax lawyer to get the IRS off my back. As luck would have it, the lawyer I hired ripped me off and never made any efforts toward remedying the situation, even after four months. Luckily, I came across a CPA, a God-send, who agreed to resolve the matter for a mere one hundred dollars - it was the only amount I could offer. In less than a month's time, my case was settled, leaving me with only the $9,700 I owed the financial institute from which I borrowed funds from my 401k. The only thing I needed to worry about was making the monthly payments negotiated in the settlement on time.

Still, try as I might, I had absolutely no idea what "happened" or from where my constant conditioning of failure had come. Even worse, I had no idea where the time, the years, the days, or the weeks had gone. Such a realization felt extremely asphyxiating. The fact that the perceived imprisonment of my circumstances had been completely created in my own mind didn't make the experience any more pleasurable. I'd done plenty of homework. I'd read every self-help book I could possibly gather from every shelf, of every bookstore I could find around the city. Yet for some reason, my subconscious reaction to previous conditioning was much more powerful and controlling than the logic-filled pages in the ever-growing pile of books sitting in the corner of my room.

Again, it was extremely challenging to comprehend how my reality (everything that occurred in those three years) resulted from one of my many attempts to step out on my own to start a business. True, I had done so without a job, or a sizeable savings to supplement my efforts, but I thought trusting in the impossible was the whole point of stepping out on faith. I could never have imagined on my worst day going through the type of hardship I faced during that period. Nor could I ever say that I grew accustomed to the struggle. Yet, it continuously confirmed just how little I valued my life, just how little I really believed in myself, and just how often I looked for the promise of change and resolution *outside* of myself, rather than *within*.

There came a point where I knew something within me had to change. If my circumstances weren't changing, then it was time to get re-acquainted with the woman in the mirror. I remember the moment I made that decision to do so, sitting in the middle of a tiny room, drowning in a sea of bewilderment, as though it happened yesterday. I was completely lost to any understanding of how I could begin letting go of the *buts* that made it impossible for me to swim toward the shore of freedom. The important thing that rings loudly when looking back to those days of hardship is the impact of striving for success while maintaining negative belief patterns about who I *thought* I was. I may have wanted to be a successful business owner, but my negative beliefs, my thoughts, my choices, and my decisions said otherwise. Despite my willingness to endeavor the path of entrepreneurship, the belief system I entertained during those days told me I was unworthy of success, ineligible for having more or better, and incapable of proving my mother and father wrong about their perception of me being a lost child who refused to find her way.

I remember growing weary of the nothingness that had been draping over me like a dirty cloak. To continue living my life in such a fashion was no longer something I was willing to do. Something had to give. Somehow, someway, I mustered up enough courage to face the success that was waiting for me on the other side of my *buts*. The light I needed to find my way through the darkness started to shine with one monumental decision: to love myself into a seeing what I was truly capable of creating through my life. So, instead of focusing on all of the torment, I opted to look for the blessings – the first being that I was still alive and *going through life*, rather than *dead*, homeless, prostituting, or addicted to drugs. I decided to focus on the fact that friends had come together to support me, even though I did whatever I could to keep them from seeing the entire story. I started changing my beliefs about who I was and who I had the potential to become. I also made a conscious choice to turn my pain into purpose. Through that choice, I was able to understand that I am meant to share love to the world by being a teacher of the lessons learned during what I previously perceived to be a horrible existence.

It was a daily effort, but I managed to change my thinking, as well as the perspective I held about *everything* that had transpired in my life and all the agony I'd been harboring up until that point. As a result of my submission, I was able to get a glimpse of the life I was meant to live and began to make my way toward it. I haven't looked back since. I was able to take all of the pain and discomfort and turn them into blessings, most of which I am able to share with others. Interestingly enough, when I found the courage to get over the shame and disappointment and started sharing what happened to me during those years with my friends, I discovered that they, too, had been through trials and tribulations in their own lives – some of them similar to mine. Yes, there are many days where I still need to remind myself to forgive, to allow myself to be healed from the mistakes, and to stop perceiving my life as wasted time. I now know in hindsight that it was only through my not-so-pleasant experiences that I was able to acquire life's greatest lessons that come with falling out of alignment with my Truth – love and belief.

Here is something else I was able to reflect on during that period: since I was a child, it seemed as though I was blessed with a surplus of energy toward which I was able to put forth into athletics since the age of 10. Though this was a deeply rooted passion, it was not my *greatest* aspiration – to be a world-renowned writer. I will be honest in admitting that from the moment I could clearly understand the dynamics and intricacies of the game, basketball became one of my first true loves – music, drawing, and writing being the others. As a young girl, never did I conceive of a day when playing basketball would come to an end. Even when I'd gotten pregnant in the middle of my sophomore year and had to drop out of college, I kept the passion for the game in one pocket and a basketball in the other. Even well into my late twenties, early thirties, not once did I ever contemplate a day where my playing days would become nonexistent. I played three to four times a week in every woman's league or tournament I could find, and on Sundays with my guy friends. I had a mediocre job, but at least my bills were paid. The only thing I cared about was playing basketball, neglecting to calculate exactly where all of the time I spent playing could potentially lead me. Yet, all the while I ignored the fervent yearning to write which I kept neatly on the backburner of my life.

Eventually, age became a factor and playing basketball had become quite a challenge, yet my fervent desire to competitively exert myself remained. For a while, I took up the seasonal game of tennis and ramped up my weekly workouts. Still, this wasn't quite enough to quell the urge to compete, succeed, and win - or at least relish in the thrill of the attempt. Fortunately, during my hardship, I discovered a path that led me right back to the game of basketball. What initially started out being a means to an end, and to put food in my stomach, became the key that would unlock the door to my potential. At the age of 41, I decided to us this period of my life to seriously embark upon the journey of becoming a Division II Women's College Basketball official. In case you haven't already figured it out, 41 years is an extremely late start for a woman interested in succeeding in this profession.

During the 6 season that I officiated, I learned how to find a certain level of balance that enabled me to hold down a full-time career as a Business Analyst (which somewhat involved my true passion of writing, but not to the degree of fulfillment), as well as the part-time avocation that involved basketball (something I most certainly love, but again, it wasn't my deepest and greatest aspiration). The road to achievement during this time was not an easy one, especially in the beginning, where I was learning a completely different side of the game I knew, loved, and played so well. *Passion* and *love* were the very motivations I needed to overcome the number of the excuses (the biggest being age) that would have hindered any probability of being successful in this venture.

However, despite my age I was able to be a rookie all over again, which ultimately gave me a brand-new perspective on how to live life and create desired results. Discomfort of being so far from realizing the end result kept me both open and eager to learn. Because of this, I was fortunate to gain a deeper understanding of who I am, who I am not, what I am made of, and what I can accomplish in my life. I found willpower. I found courage. I found self-love and compassion – for fellow officials, as well as athletes, clinicians, coaches, administrators, and of course, me. Individuals who have ever pursued the path of becoming a professional official can relate to the strenuous and arduous tasks that come with climbing the ladder of success in that industry - especially as a female. Criticism, scrutiny, and high degrees of judgment are something we experience each time we step on a court. It can be extremely grueling and not everyone is cut out for the type of work that far exceeded the adjudication of rules. Still, traversing the path of excellence in this field could not have been possible without first learning to manage my time, my emotions, my self-image, my relationships (with significant others, supervisors, players, coaches, and crew members), my thoughts, my beliefs, my ambition for success in my career, and my ability to reach goals and aspirations.

Finally, as I am closing out my last year on the court to pursue my passion as a writer with a purpose of inspiring women to love themselves into full potential, the most peculiar reality presented itself to me: the same competitive edge or energy maintained in the realm of athletics was not applied to my desire to maintain loving relationships – with me and with others. Nor was it applied toward my ambition to reach success as a writer at my highest potential. I realize now that the essentials I acquired in my determination to succeed as an official at a late stage in life, are the very things that were lacking earlier in my life that I feel would have impelled me to follow my dreams with much more fervency and much sooner.

As you can see, I have chased many aspirations to the best of my ability throughout my life. Yet, I am still not able to say that I did so with the same tenacious vigor for achievement into them as I had with officiating. While looking back at all of my creative ventures, success seemed to have been disguised – at least from a notoriety and revenue generating perspective. Eventually, I figured out that employing the same energies and exertions I had towards athletics into my aspirations would bring me greater results in the area of dream realization. Whereas my love and passion for basketball compelled me to reach new heights (much like the urgency of winning in competition since the age of 10), I had neglected to direct my passion for writing and teaching toward the prevailing of excuses that prohibited me from the success I deserved and desired. That is, until now (at the time of writing this book).

I hope you can garner encouragement from the shared experience of being "sick and tired" of mediocrity or allowing past failures and negative belief patterns to impede progress in life. There are always moments that arise to provoke us to get still and to listen for the echo of our Truth that will lead us back into alignment with purpose and meaning. There is always a blessing woven within each trial. There is always an opportunity for growth and evolution. We must be reminded to see beyond our circumstances, and to know that somewhere within us lies the strength and courage needed to love ourselves, to place the same amount (if not more) of worthiness on our own desires as we do on the desires of others; to be a humble servant of our gifts and talents, and to find meaning and purpose in our dreams and aspirations. Because of this, I was able to remain focused, committed and dedicated to accomplishing the goal of becoming a Division II Women's College Basketball official. I finally did it! Now I have beneath me a platform on which to stand that justifies my ability to believe in possibility and reaching my highest potential.

♥♥♥♥♥

Having picked up this book and made it this far along, the assumption is that each of us has accepted that a need for change in our lives has surfaced. Let us make sure we stand tall and confident, even in the midst of uncertainty, pain, and confusion. Let's choose love as we rise out of the perception of limiting circumstances and conditions. Let's brush each other off and encourage one another to grab hold of the power nestled deep within our hearts. Let's tell our stories without guilt, judgment, or regret. Today, we shall embrace the will to let go of our excuses so that we may transition from the past into our current moment, where we can continue to discover the gift of wisdom. Let us accept and be grateful for our current circumstances, no matter what degree of difficulty they appear. For without them we would not be capable of becoming more of who we really are. Let us have trust, faith, purpose, and meaning behind our dreams and aspirations as we prepare to venture into the realm of all possibility and pure potential.

Before we take our first step toward love together, there is one thing we must do. As difficult as it may seem, let us do our best to jump out of our minds and into our spirit. Our minds, where our thoughts, beliefs, and perceptions are generated, are what have gotten us to where we are in this moment. Let us begin to trust that the love, purpose, and passion residing in our hearts will help us sustain and persevere through tough times. Letting go of excuses and justifications for shortcomings, and allowing the spirit within to guide us, will align us with the things and people we need to reach the fruition of our greatest aspirations. Our spirits will provide us with the patience and peace that are essential to staying the course. The spirit within will remind us of a love and purpose behind our dreams that is much bigger than who we are in this moment.

Remember, it is impossible for love and fear to exist in the same space. We must choose to live *from* the space of love so that fear can no longer imprison us. Thus, it is essential that we take the time to heal the wounds of our past in order to surrender our excuses.

Know that the Universe is always revealing to us signs and conspiring with our internal request to evolve and grow. Developing our self-awareness and increasing our self-love will make it easier to recognize the signs that will propel us forward by way of making healthier choices and wiser decisions. Understand that the time to evolve is always in the present moment - not in the past, and not in the future, but right now.

We must strive to change our perspective of what is occurring and always seek the best outcome; otherwise, we run the risk of missing the pathway leading us to our next level of success or fulfillment. Let's avoid getting distracted by ill-favored circumstances that appear not to be working in our favor. Trusting that everything is working out for "our own good" helps with maintaining the type of optimistic outlook that enables us to recognize the time to release and then move forward and upward from our present circumstances, without regret or criticism. Let us choose the mindset of healing.

If you agree, take a deep breath and exhale all of the worry, all of the pain, and all of the doubt and negative beliefs. While doing so, embrace every desire, every dream, every idea, and every thought you ever had about your success and desire for fulfillment. The truth of the matter is that you can never and will never stop growing and expanding. You are either choosing to do so willingly, lovingly, joyfully, compassionately, and peacefully, or you are doing so begrudgingly, unwillingly, and fearfully. Assuming you are making the decision today, in the here and now, to embark upon your designated journey with an outlook of exhilaration and excitement, I encourage you to lean into who you really are, into your true potential, and into love while shouting at the top of your lungs:

I love who I am! I already am and have whatever I need to be exactly as I envision. And now… I give myself permission to achieve!

As cliché and "happy-ending-ish" as this may sound, I assure you that today I live life striving to meet my greatest and highest potential. I needed that "valley" experience in order to recognize that it was time for me to move forward and upward into my next level of existence. Instead of wallowing in despair, I was able to stop, breathe, and bring myself into alignment with what is true for my life, and for me. I fervently desire to be a guiding light to help you accomplish the same. I believe that the purpose behind the crossing of our paths is so that I might share with you the very gift of revelation to which I have been bestowed. This would be a feat I could never accomplish had I never let go of my *but* several years prior, if I never deemed my life and my dreams worthy of the same exertion I placed toward any endeavor pertaining to basketball. It is my hope that you too will comprehend how letting go of your *buts* and loving your way into true potential will prove to be the most rewarding decision you make in your life.

Enjoy the journey!

Continuing the Course

I am optimistic that we are now collectively inspired to unearth the willpower and longing for self-actualization nestled deep inside each of our hearts. I am even more confident that we are also charged with the responsibility of aiming for our desired goals and dreams. Because we have chosen to love ourselves into possibility and potential, we are now equipped to answer the call on our lives. For this, I must say, we should be very proud. In this moment, let us relish in this enthusiasm. As we continue to support each other in our endeavor to grow and nurture ourselves toward achievement and fulfillment, we shall remain humble and encouraged to see every circumstance that arises, and every person we encounter, through the lens of love. We shall strive to recognize and remember the honor of having the creative aptitude to bring forth (both literally and figuratively) something new, something great, which can only be bred through us, as we are in this moment. We shall courageously accept that we have each arrived at the point in our lives where we are ready to consciously become the personification of the self we envision.

As we close out this chapter of our journey together, and prepare to open the next, let us remember to be of service to others beyond our current needs. Let us strive daily to remind each other to stay encouraged, to remain focused, to be authentic, to keep our hearts and minds open and available to possibility, and (most importantly) to continue cultivating the path of evolution and creativity.

Whatever, whenever, and however we choose to step forward into our greatness, I gently suggest that we keep one thing in mind: *going against the common grain of mediocrity, commonly known as "the road less traveled," is a complicated and arduous a feat.* Do not be discouraged. Simply choose the path of least resistance, which entails letting go of the excuses that hinder progress. Remember that preparation is key. Being inspired by the context written on the pages of this book is one thing, while turning inspiration into action is a completely different chore all together. Though no one has ever proclaimed that the road to success is an easy one, there is a beautiful and gratifying restitution for those of us who choose to traverse it. To live beyond our feelings about what occurred in our past, or is occurring in the present moment, and decide to move faithfully toward a more loving possibility will be extremely challenging, initially. Yet, each and every one of us is worthy of making the effort. Trusting ourselves to stay in the position of alignment with what we aspire for our lives, even in spite of the contrasting circumstances that surround us, is one of the hardest things we will ever have to do. Maintaining exhilaration, fervency, and determination in a society seething with distractions, confusion, and destruction is something we are going to have to re-learn. Provision won't always be evident, yet staying, standing, and stepping into what is true for us with a level of assurance that all is well, and all is good, is imperative in the pursuit of freedom, fruition, and achievement.

What I am really attempting to drive home is that change is inevitable. We must be mindful of how we are choosing to transcend the challenges that are forcing us to make the necessary transitions that will ultimately lead us toward a preferred outcome. At the end of each day, when the awareness that we made it through the obstacle course of opposition finally hits us, we can exhale and express gratitude for the blessings, opportunities, and choices that stand before us as a result. Instead of being draped in fear, we will lovingly remind ourselves of our potential. Thus, we face the next day with a sense of knowing because we have chosen to remain prepared, focused, and aligned with whatever experiences we desire. We understand that the journey for us does not stop here, and that our current circumstances can *never* dictate who we are. Because of this, we will fulfill our promise to continue the course and "do the work" it takes to realize our greatest potential.

To assist us with this process of evolution, I have listed a few tips for our reference below:

- We will surround ourselves with people, circumstances, and environments that are conducive for growth and achievement.
- We will seek love, motivation, and inspiration in every relationship or situation we encounter.

- Email the Author:
  - Naje Badu: NajeBadu@gmail.com or visit www.NajeBadu.com
  - Share stories of achievement and success.
  - Share other women's stories of inspiration that will us to continue our perspective paths.

- Share challenges and request insight to help with overcoming fear and discouragement.
- Seek counsel and guidance:
  - Partner with a mentor.
  - Partner with a counselor or life coach.

And lastly, here are five ways to increase our chances of overcoming impediments and excuses:

1. Know thyself, love thyself - until we know who we are, or until we can love ourselves without apology, we will never come to know our strengths and weaknesses. Therefore, we must always be accountable for our choices and decisions and remain true to ourselves, always and in all ways.
2. Give the light within us permission to shine and inspire others to do the same, no matter what is, or is not occurring in our lives.
3. Allow negative people or situations to be the sandpaper that refines the aspects of who we are that requires smoothing, refinement, or enhancement.
4. Perceive adversities and opposition as conduits designed to lead us toward our destiny and propel us into promotion.
5. Believe that life is happening *for* us, rather than *to* us.

Again, our journey together does not stop here. We have much more to discover, learn, and experience together. For now, I'd like to take the opportunity to thank each of you for sharing your time and energy and allowing me the space to do the same.

Remember: *Limitations and boundaries do not exist unless you create them.*

For the sake of encouraging you to create new possibilities, I urge you to reach out and learn more about the benefits of coaching (individual or group). If you have been greatly inspired, consider passing along what you have shared with others, including organizations, businesses, or teams that may benefit from guidance and insight offered through the principles shared within this book. Otherwise, I look forward to connecting with you in Volume II of this series.

Just a quick reminder: make sure to attend future *Let Go of Your But!* seminars, workshops, or online courses, all of which are specifically designed and constructed to guide women to love themselves fully and unapologetically. The intention behind each of the *Let Go of Your But!* events is to help women realize their dreams and aspirations at full potential. Attending any one of these events will certainly leave you inspired and empowered to start courageously and excitedly creating the life you aspire to have. You will also be ignited to realize the deepest, truest aspect of who you really are. You will be moved to become all you were designed to become so that you may have and experience everything you desire and envision. Stop by the NajeBadu.com to contact me, learn about where and when I will be speaking live, or find out more about upcoming *Let Go of Your But!* events in your area.

About the Author

SELF-LOVE IS a KEY TO SUCCESS - "If you truly like yourself, you will never run out of good friends. If you love yourself, you can love anyone in the world. If you love the world, you can embrace and accept the Spirit that lives in all things – including you."

— Naje Badu

Naje Badu (formerly known as Kimberly E. Banks) was raised in Los Angeles, California.

Ms. Badu's mission is focused on creating a collection of works that centers on elevating women, as well as, uplifting the human spirit as a whole. Ms. Badu's sole desire is to write content that provokes readers to be accountable for their lives and arriving to their intended destinations; to search deep within their souls in order to find ways to contribute to the healing of our society.

With a background in psychology, spirituality and serving as a professional success/life coach, she is inclined to inspire readers to believe that they too can make it through dark days to see the brighter. Each project (both inspirational and nonfiction) the author pens teach life lessons centered on compassion, perseverance, acceptance, and humility. Encouraging readers to tap into their own gifts, talent and passions in their quest for love and fulfillment is Naje's life purpose.

Talent Management

TheRhyze! Inc.

Website: www.TheRhyze.com

Artist Representation:

Angela Burris
Email: Angela@TheRhyze.com
Phone: (323) 572 - 5944

Author Representation

Sonya Patton
Email: SPatton@TheRhyze.com
Phone: (857) 212 - 1897

www.ingramcontent.com/pod-product-compliance
Lightning Source LLC
Chambersburg PA
CBHW060353110426
42743CB00036B/2875